Narrative Practice

Narrative Practice

CONTINUING THE CONVERSATIONS

Michael White

Edited by David Denborough

Preface
Jill Freedman

Introduction
David Epston

Epilogue
Cheryl White

Postscript and Acknowledgment
Cheryl White

W. W. NORTON & COMPANY
NEW YORK • LONDON

For information about permission to reproduce selections
from this book, write to Permissions,
W. W. Norton & Company, Inc., 500 Fifth Avenue, New York, NY 10110

For information about special discounts for bulk purchases,
please contact W. W. Norton Special Sales at
specialsales@wwnorton.com or 800-233-4830

Manufacturing by RR Donnelley, Bloomsburg
Book design by Joe Lops
Production manager: Leeann Graham

Library of Congress Cataloging-in-Publication Data

White, Michael (Michael Kingsley)
Narrative practice : continuing the conversations / Michael White ; edited by
David Denborough ; preface, Jill Freedman ; introduction, David Epston ;
epilogue, Cheryl White ; postscript and acknowledgment,
Cheryl White. — 1st ed.
p. ; cm.
"A Norton Professional Book."
Includes bibliographical references and index.
ISBN 978-0-393-70692-5 (hardcover)
1. Narrative therapy. 2. Psychotherapy. I. Denborough, David. II. Title.
[DNLM: 1. Psychotherapy—methods. 2. Narration. WM 420]
RC489.S74W46 2011
616.89'165—dc22
2010041788

ISBN: 978-0-393-70692-5

W. W. Norton & Company, Inc.,
500 Fifth Avenue, New York, N.Y. 10110
www.wwnorton.com

W. W. Norton & Company Ltd., Castle House,
75/76 Wells Street, London W1T 3QT

4 5 6 7 8 9 0

Contents

Acknowledgments

We would like to acknowledge the W. W. Norton staff in assisting us to bring this book to publication. Deborah Malmud's enthusiasm and editorial input have been invaluable and Margaret Ryan's copyediting skills have made a significant contribution to this manuscript. Mark Trudinger also provided editorial assistance.

We would also like to acknowledge Mary Heath and Rachel Herzing, who provided valuable feedback on earlier drafts of Chapter 7.

Finally, we would like to thank the following practitioners, who responded to our invitation to contribute to the Epilogue: Isabelle Laplante (France), Nicolas De Beer (France), Niels-Henrik Sørensen (Denmark), John Stillman (USA), Jim Duvall (Canada), Caleb Wakhungu (Uganda), Leticia Uribe (Mexico), Marilene Grandesso (Brazil), Pierre Blanc-Sahnoun (France), Maggie Carey (Australia), Yishai Shalif (Israel), Sekneh Hammoud-Beckett (Australia), Walter Bera (USA), Gaye Stockell (Australia), Alfonso Diaz-Smith (Mexico), Hugh Fox (UK), Shona Russell (Australia), Geir Lundby (Norway), Tod Augusta-Scott (Canada), John Winslade (NZ/USA), Jonathan Morgan (South Africa), Peggy Sax (USA), Sarah Hughes (Canada), Maksuda Begum (Bangladesh), Rudi Kronbichler (Austria), Ruth Pluznick (Canada), Zoy Kazan (USA), Marilyn O'Neill (Australia), Yasunaga Komori (Japan), Lorraine

Hedtke (USA), Vivian Navartnam (Singapore), Cuqui Toledo (Mexico), Kaethe Weingarten (USA), Jeff Zimmerman (USA), Angela Tsun on-Kee (Hong Kong), Maria Angela Teixeira (Brazil), Daria Kutuzova (Russia/France), Angel Yuen (Canada), and Chris Beels (USA).

Editor's Note

David Denborough

Ohe story within this book is particularly significant to me. In Chapter 2 Michael relays a story about Donna, whom he first met when her parents were very concerned about her quality of life. Donna had a diagnosis of schizophrenia, had been on medication for this for several years, and had experienced a number of admissions to a psychiatric hospital. Michael had a series of meetings with Donna and her family over a period of 8 months, and during this time she began to step into the world. For many years, however, Donna would still occasionally visit Michael at Dulwich Centre for what she referred to as a "top-up." On one particular day, the meeting took an unexpected turn:

> On this occasion of meeting with Donna, I hadn't seen her for 5 months. At the end of our conversation, she looked around my interviewing room, took in the surroundings with a studied eye, and exclaimed: "What a mess!" She was mostly referring to my filing system—at the time I had a horizontal filing system and could never find what I was looking for. My response: "Yes, it really is a mess. And I am determined to do something about this." Donna's response: "What makes you think that you are ready to take this step?" There was something ever so familiar about this question. I laughed, and did my best to respond. Then, a further question from Donna: "I guess this decision

didn't come out of the blue. What led up to it?" Now we were both laughing. Donna continued to scaffold this interview with questions like: "When do you think that you will be ready to take this step?" "Sometime in the next week or two, I guess," I said.

We chatted some more, and I then accompanied Donna down to the reception area. There, to my surprise, Donna made another appointment to meet with me, this time in 2 weeks. I remarked that this was a departure from her habit of leaving it until she felt that she needed another top-up. "Oh," Donna responded enthusiastically, "This appointment is not for me, it's for you! I have made a time for you to see me in 2 weeks to see how you went with this plan to fix up your mess." I was open-mouthed.

Donna had made the appointment time for early on a Thursday morning, and I was up half the night on Wednesday getting my filing system into a vertical format. I then managed a few hours sleep, before fortifying myself with caffeine ahead of my meeting with Donna. It was a fantastic event. Donna dramatically swept into my room ahead of me and loudly proclaimed: "What a change! You really got it together!" Then she paused: "But I shouldn't say that. It is what you think of this that counts." We were again laughing together, with Donna making it even more difficult for me to collect myself by asking questions like, "How does this affect your picture of yourself?"

This story is significant to me for a number of reasons. It conveys something of the delight, mirth, and egalitarian politics that accompanied Michael's therapeutic practice, particularly with people with serious mental health concerns. It also offers a glimpse as to the task of putting together this collection of Michael's unpublished works. If it hadn't been for Donna, perhaps we wouldn't have found some of the chapters of *this* book! As it was, last summer was spent immersed within Michael's horizontal and vertical filing systems. It also involved foraging amidst piles of floppy disks: those archaic plastic disks that make a whirring sound so evocative of the 1980s and 1990s. There must have been over 200 of these. The process felt a little bit like a rescue mission. I never knew what discovery might be just around the corner.

And indeed gems were found. Many of the manuscripts I already knew about and was deliberately looking for, but others were unexpected. I'd open the 17th file on a particular floppy disk (always the files were labeled in incomprehensible ways) and suddenly here were previously unknown stories and sparkling ideas. It was an exhilarating feeling, and one I had known so many times before.

January was always Michael's writing time. In the heat of summer, he would be tucked away reading and writing. We'd wait patiently and gently inquire about how things were going. And then the first draft would be ready and handed to me. I always so looked forward to this moment. I always knew that Michael's latest stories and ideas would make me think differently about life. They always did. And then we would work together to bring them to their final form.

And so this time around, searching amidst the filing systems, it was as if I came across 11 first drafts. Some were much more complete than others. In compiling writings after an author's death, it seems important to be transparent about the work that has taken place behind the scenes.

Here, I offer a little history about each chapter and explain what work was required on each of them to publish them here.

1. Bringing the World into Therapy and Subverting the Operations of Modern Power

This chapter, which provides an engaging introduction to Michael's unique perspectives on modern power and their implications for therapy, has been constructed from two different sources: a keynote address that Michael gave at the 2nd

Dulwich Centre International Narrative Therapy and Community Work Conference, which was held in Adelaide in 2000; and workshop notes from 1999 entitled "Different Faces of Power."

2. Turning Points and the Significance of Personal and Community Ethics

Michael presented this moving, amusing, and inspiring keynote address at the Dulwich Centre International Summer School of Narrative Practice in Adelaide in 2004. A small extract from a manuscript note entitled "making it more difficult to be ethical" has also been included.

3. Power, Psychotherapy, and New Possibilities for Dissent

How can therapists refuse to reproduce the dominant culture in therapy? In this chapter, Michael seeks to provide a way beyond an ethic of control. It is an extract from a longer manuscript prepared for a conference held in Adelaide. Written in the early 1990s, this paper required minimal editing.

4. "Countertransference" and Rich Story Development

5. The Resistances and Therapist Responsibility

Canvassing topics that Michael rarely spoke about—the phenomena of "countertransference" and "resistance"—these two chapters were drawn from presentations that Michael gave at the Evolution of Psychotherapy Conference in Anaheim, in 2005. Both of these chapters combine the notes that Michael had developed for these presentations with the stories he told at the conference. The stories were transcribed and woven into the text.

6. On Anorexia: An Interview

It has been many years since Michael last published his thoughts relating to narrative responses to anorexia. I conducted this interview with Michael in the Melbourne airport in May 2006. We had sent it to a number of practitioners for review in 2007 but had never got around to publishing it. It required only minor proofreading changes prior to inclusion here.

7. The Responsibilities: Working with Men Who Have Perpetrated Violence

In 2005 and 2006, Michael held two special intensives on the topic of "Responding to Violence." In preparation for these workshops, Michael and I met with WOWSAFE (a women's group working to address men's violence against women) and with men in the Violence Prevention Unit at Long Bay Prison at the invitation of Rachael Haggett. This chapter has been constructed from a number of different sources: notes that Michael wrote and distributed during the Responding to Violence workshop in 2006; three separate sets of handwritten workshop notes that Michael had kept in a folder in relation to this topic that outlined a "map" for separating from abusive ways of being; a therapeutic letter written by Michael in 2001; and a therapeutic letter that Michael and I cowrote after visiting Long Bay Prison in 2006. I first attended training at Dulwich Centre 17 years ago while seeking to respond to men's violence in my job at Long Bay Prison and also with young men in schools. I believe that the implications of Michael's ideas in relation to responding to men's violence are highly significant. Having been in conversations with Michael about responding to men's violence since the early 1990s, it is with some sense of relief that these ideas are now available to practitioners.

8. Externalizing and Responsibility

One of the most common questions Michael was asked in workshops was "How does the concept of externalizing relate to considerations of responsibility?" This chapter provides a response. It is an edited transcript from a presentation Michael gave at the Evolution of Psychotherapy Conference in Anaheim, in 2005.

9. Revaluation and Resonance: Narrative Responses to Traumatic Experience

In the early 2000s, Michael's attention was drawn to exploring narrative responses to trauma, and he presented an influential keynote address on this theme at Dulwich Centre's 4th International Narrative Therapy and Community Work Conference in Atlanta, Georgia, in 2002. In the lead-up to the conference, Michael wrote a number of versions of this presentation, all of which had far more material than he could present in that forum. Within one of the versions, I found these detailed notes on "revaluation and resonance." It was necessary to include within this chapter an extract of text explaining the concept of the "absent but implicit." This extract is taken from a previously published piece by Michael (2003).

10. Engagements with Suicide

Responding to those who have lost loved ones to suicide was a topic Michael taught but did not publish on during his lifetime. This chapter was constructed from three different sources: a manuscript dated 15th October 1999 provides the introduction; an edited transcript from a video recording in the Michael White Archive provides the example of practice (identifying details have been changed); and the joining paragraph and conclusion have been reconstructed from workshop notes.

11. Couples Therapy: Entering Couples into an Adventure

Therapists routinely request further ideas about narrative ways of working with couples. Because of this, we have included these undated notes, which we found amidst Michael's files. They were probably written in 1999 or 2000.

Eleven chapters, eleven gems. Each in their own way illuminates an aspect of Michael's diverse contributions to the field of therapeutic practice.

Michael was fond of quoting Clifford Geertz about the importance of "rescuing the said from the saying of it" (see Geertz, 1983; Newman, 2008). The spoken word is ephemeral; it does not last. So when a person articulates hard-won knowledge about his or her life, it can be the role of the therapist to "rescue" *what* was said, and the *meaning* of what was said, and to document this in ways that the person can examine in the future and put to continuing use in his or her life. This process involves both honoring and extending the "life" of words that otherwise may pass unnoticed. How this process unfolds involves ethical considerations at every step of the way.

I have approached the task of editing the eleven chapters that appear in this collection as an act of "rescue"—an act of recovery or preservation from loss. Each time I came across a file on one of those floppy disks, it was with exhilaration but also with a sense of "how easily this could have been lost." This book seeks to honor and extend the life of words that otherwise may have passed unnoticed, and to preserve these in a form that makes it possible for future therapists to put them to use.

Along the way, we have tried to consider the multiple ethical considerations of working with the words of someone who has passed away. Significantly, all the original fragments and writings that represent the "draft" chapters of this book will be held in the Michael White Archive so that future scholars, if they so wish, will be able to consider and trace every edit and reconstruction of text that was involved in putting together this collection.

Just the other day, I called Donna because I wanted to let her know about this book. Donna said how pleased she was to hear about this. She also spoke about how much she cared for Michael and how she missed him. When I reminded her about her efforts to assist Michael in tidying the mess of his office, and how these had made the process of putting together this book just a little easier, we both laughed.

The sound of laughter was heard quite regularly coming out of Michael's therapy room. I hope its echoes are found within the pages of this book.

Preface

Jill Freedman

once jokingly told Michael that I was mad at him. I explained that it all started when I was rereading one of his papers. I indignantly asked him how he had managed to sneak my latest new idea into a paper he had written 6 years earlier and that I had read carefully when it was first published. He grinned and apologized!

Michael's writings are always full of new ideas, no matter how many times I read them and no matter how long ago they were written. This has been a comfort to me since his death. I can reread and reread and always find something new. But what a gift to have a book of his writing never before published. This book is a treasure trove that I know I will explore for years to come.

One of the gifts is the inclusion of papers that were originally given as plenary addresses. It is an unexpected pleasure and great source of learning for those of us who heard these inspirational addresses to be able to go back over them slowly and study them. For those who were not present when Michael gave the addresses, here is a second chance.

Michael's descriptions of his work with a number of people are also included in the book. In these descriptions we are treated not only to the details of his work, but we see the exquisite care he took in his therapy relationships. I was so glad to see that the book includes a lengthy transcript. This is the closest we can come in book form to witnessing Michael at work.

There are also essays that immerse us in the complexity of his thinking and the commitments and purposes that always supported his work. His words about ethics and politics are straightforward and clear: " . . . it is never a matter of whether or not we bring politics into the therapy room, but whether or not we are prepared to acknowledge the existence of these politics, and the degree to which we are prepared to be complicit in the reproduction of these politics."

Perhaps because this is Michael's last book, I decided to savor it slowly, reading a small section each morning in my therapy room before the day's conversations began. These pages had me laughing and in tears. They also gave me new inspiration in my work. I noticed moments in my conversations with the people who were consulting me that resonated with scenes Michael described. I could feel myself responding differently in my work, in ways that I felt good about. When I read Michael's words, " . . . perhaps it is now time for us to find new ways of recuperating statements of conscious purpose, and to elevate these statements so that they are more constitutive of our lives and our work," I found myself crying out "Yes!"

It is a joy to hear Michael's voice again. And his voice is loud and clear, soft and questioning, laughing and serious in this book. I received the book in manuscript before it had a title. I was delighted to later find that I was reading *Narrative Practice: Continuing the Conversations*. Reading it does feel like engaging in continuing conversations with Michael. But it feels like more than conversations. Through reading this book, I had the experience that Michael was joining me in my work. I wish that experience for all of the readers of this book. You couldn't have a teammate who could offer more creative and thoughtful ideas and who would more enthusiastically join in your conversations.

For a while Michael repeated a quotation about ripples that went something like this: "Those ripples that last the longest last longer than those ripples that don't last so long." I love this quotation, not only because I hear it in Michael's Australian accent but also because it speaks of small actions having bigger and bigger effects in ways that are unpredictable. Michael writes explicitly about this usefulness of noticing small actions in one of the essays in this book. This practice has always been important in his work. We see it again and again in his examples. But I mention this quotation also because of the ripples I imagine this book setting in motion. I know that those of us who have studied Michael's work and read his previous books will welcome this one. I also hope a new generation of therapists is introduced to his work through it. And I will be excited to witness the ripples.

I read this book slowly the first time through but have already gone back to it again and again. I have starred pages and written myself notes and underlined sentences. Here is one of the notes I scrawled in the margin: "This raises questions for me—I would love to talk about with Michael. Instead, we'll just have to talk with each other." And I fervently hope that we do.

Introduction

David Epston

Michael, I read a short story some months after you died, and I know it struck me like a blow in my undefended solar plexus.

A bartender was the narrator of this story. He told of a patron coming day after day, sitting on the identical bar stool and ordering the same two glasses of white wine. The bartender knew not to interrupt, as his customer was engaged in what appeared to him to be earnest conversation with an unseen interlocutor. After finishing both glasses of wine in an hour or more, he would take his leave. After several years during which they had become accustomed to each other, the bartender was emboldened to ask, "Why two glasses of wine instead of one?" His customer sorrowfully confided in him that the other glass was for his friend who had had to seek political exile. Some months later, his customer ordered a single glass. The bartender did something he never did; he reached across the bar and touched him, saying "My condolences" (Galeano, 2006, p. 213).

Michael, with what you have left behind and particularly the two hoards—these caches of treasures, one of which includes the papers that follow in this text and your archive of video-tapes (go to http://www.dulwichcentre.com.au/michael-white-archive.html)—I can imagine that many of us will set out two glasses, one for you and one for ourselves. We have so much more to speak to you about, and you have so much more to say to us.

I started writing this Introduction on April 4, the second anniversary of your sudden death. I think it was unwise of me to do so, as I found myself writing something akin to my earlier obituary. This precipitated a turmoil of sleepless nights and disturbed days. I took some comfort from Joan Didion: "Grief turns out to be a place none of us know until we reach it" (2003, p. 188). And some weeks later, when I returned to the project, I seemed even further away from knowing how to proceed. Perturbed, I turned to Ann (Epston), as you know I do. "Why don't you write a letter to Michael?"[1] My spirits immediately lifted, as I had so much I had wanted to speak to you about, and now I could have the means to do so—much like the patron ordering two glasses of white wine instead of the customary one.

You will remember, Michael, how we both had finally settled on a date to reunite in Adelaide, after several previous cancellations. Now we had no doubt that nothing could or would get in the way of this assignation. Lamentably, that day turned out to be merely three weeks after you died. My return to Adelaide was for your funeral. I can't tell you how much I was anticipating such a rendezvous to chart the course of the next phase of our "brotherhood of ideas" in to our respective dotages.

Since the mid-1990s, we had had to regretfully acknowledge that, despite our best intentions, our respective work lives and travel commitments had ruled this out. Do you recall our continual astonishment at how narrative therapy took off after our preconference workshop at the 1989 American Association for Marriage and Family Therapy (AAMFT) Conference in San Francisco and your live interview with the so-called "firelighter"—and then the special issue on narrative therapy in the *Family Therapy Networker* in 1994 (Simon, 1994), and a year later, the *Newsweek* article (Cowley & Springen, 1995)? And, more recently, both of us had busied ourselves in our respective writing projects—Rick Maisel and I co-authoring *Biting the Hand That Starves You: Inspiring Resistance to Anorexia/Bulimia* (Maisel, Epston, & Borden, 2004), while you were working on *Maps of Narrative Practice* (White, 2007). Michael, did you have some foreknowledge of your untimely death that you worked so hard preparing what I consider to be a distillate of your life's work?

It has now come to mean so much to me that I launched your *Maps* book at the International Conference in Kristiansand in Norway.[2] And I am laughing to myself how when you learned I was scheduled to do so, you used every ounce of your considerable powers of persuasion to convince me to call it off. When you could see how unyielding I remained, you came up with some specious arguments. Michael, for one who was so reverent and acknowledging of everyone who crossed your path in your workplaces or throughout your life and who had given such thought to "forums" of acknowledgment (see White, 1997/2000), it was a rare occasion for us to arrange something of that sort for you.

Michael, I can't tell you how relieved I am by these unpublished papers, addresses, workshop handouts, letters, and fragments coming to light. Of course, I had known that another hoard existed in the form of videotapes. Although you had published consistently through Dulwich Centre Publications from the early 1980s onwards (Epston & White, 1992; White, 1989b, 1995a, 1997, 2000b, 2004; White & Morgan, 2006), I lamented the fact—and you shared my concerns—that you were almost exclusively referenced by *Narrative Means to Therapeutic Ends* (White & Epston, 1990) by North American scholars and practitioners.

How often did you and I talk together about how we both owed such an enormous debt to the independence of Cheryl White, Jane Hales, David Denborough, and Mark Trudinger at Dulwich Centre Publications? Their publications have engaged with so much of what concerned you, Michael. No mainstream publisher could or would have been able to publish many of their titles. Dulwich Centre Publications has been, and will continue to be, the primary "voice" of narrative therapy and community work for some time to come. And to think it all began in the early 1980s with a newssheet entitled "Coming Events" to announce forthcoming Friday-after-work talks at Dulwich Centre in Adelaide. Without an independent press, I believe narrative therapy would never have been able to speak as forcefully as it has in its own manner or to its numerous concerns, for some of which you were the spokesperson.

Michael, I know you were as grateful as I was to W. W. Norton, a venerable publishing house who took our modest first version (*Literary Means to Therapeutic Ends*) from "down under," renamed it (*Narrative Means to Therapeutic Ends*) and brought it to the attention of an "up over" international readership.

Susan Barrows Munro became a friend, confidante, and editor until Deborah Malmud took over from her and shepherded *Biting the Hand that Starves You* (2004) and your *Maps of Narrative Practice* (2007) through to publication. We have both taken great pride in our association with W. W. Norton.

There was such a vast territory of social, political, and ethical concerns with which you, personally, and your writings and practice were attempting to reckon. Reading across these unpublished papers will provide for those who had been unaware of these concerns some sense of your erudition, elegance of thought, generosity of spirit, and, most obviously, the courage of your convictions. And you were not alone in these convictions. You had no doubt that Cheryl was what you often referred to as "my muse," and The Family Centre (Warihi Campbell, Taimalieutu Kiwi Tamasese, Flora Tuhaka, and Charles Waldegrave) and their "Just Therapy" mentored and consulted with you as you began to engage with cultures other than your own (Waldegrave, 2005, 2009; Waldegrave, Tamasese, Tuhaka, & Campbell,

2003). And there were many others. What a reader coming to you after reading *Maps* alone can start to grasp from the range of these previously unpublished papers might be referred to as your reimagination of the "social imaginary" (Taylor, 2007, p. 171).[3] Why do I suggest such grand terms? I do so, with some reserve, to indicate your vision, even if you restricted yourself to the local and particular about life.

POETICS ALONGSIDE POLITICS

These papers direct our attention to your politics and ethics, but you rarely commented on what I am calling the *poetics* of either your practice or your thinking in general. Perhaps for you, it was so taken for granted that it was just beside the point or tacit and beyond your own telling. Anyone who watched a videotape, read a text of yours, or heard you speak couldn't help but marvel at the eloquence of your thought. Stephen Madigan mentioned to me recently that often when he would read you, "I was brought to tears . . . tears of awestruck joy very much like reading poetry, very much when one is struck with an overwhelming beauty" (S. Madigan, personal communication, April 19, 2010).

No one could plagiarize you, Michael, because your fingerprints were over everything you said or wrote. Surely you must have added several hundred questions to the library of therapy inquiry? And how many of your neologisms will turn up some day in the *Oxford English Dictionary*? In the period between 1981 and 1986, you were turning Batesonian grand theory into a practice of therapy that was entirely unique. But what was so fascinating about such an enterprise was your reworking of language so as to "get around" or circumscribe the complexities of relationship—something English cannot adequately do. It was here and in the enchanting externalizing conversations with young people that I first marveled at your genius with your vocabularies.[4] It was rare for you to say much that you had not previously invented.

Michael, don't you think we have to turn to poetics for this? After all, your words were at times mesmerizing, and it was no surprise to me that you drew upon Bachelard (1958/1994) and the aesthetic metaphor of "transport" as images for your narrative practice.

If we are to engage with the significance of poetics in narrative practice, I suspect we would have to trouble ourselves and read beyond our disciplines. Why do I believe this would be worthwhile doing? Because, Michael, it is of concern to all of us—and one which will delight us as well—to consider the language by which you brought the world of your reimagined social imaginary into view. This would cause us to reconsider externalizing conversations and perhaps make more of them than we have done so far.

In *The Language of Inquiry,* Lyn Hejinian wrote: "It is at least in part for this reason that poetry has its capacity for poetics, for self-reflexivity, for speaking about itself; it is by virtue of this that poetry can turn language upon itself and thus exceed its own limits" (Hejinian, 2000, p. 1). Poetics as well as narrative renders language a medium for experiencing experience.[5] You and those you consulted as a therapist or taught seemed provisioned to "think otherwise"—to go beyond the linguistic limits that had previously circumscribed them. I observed so many of those who consulted you from behind a one-way screen; I can think of only a very few who were not at first surprised but then delighted by where such a conversation had taken them—to have gone beyond where they had been. They were left with an inquiry of their own to think on and live their lives into—of taking a chance of "becoming another" with the implicit understanding that "this is happening."

Does this remind you of our fascination with performative ritual and your carefully crafted reworking of Myerhoff's definitional ceremony and "outsider witnessing" (Myerhoff, 1982; White, 1995b)? When we were planning to meet again, you alluded to some matters we had read in the past that we should review. Did you have van Gennep's "liminal phase" and Turner's "anti-structure" on your mind? I know I had Norman Denzin's (2003) *Performance Ethnography: Critical Pedagogy and the Politics of Culture* on my list to read with you and see what relevance it might have.

FOUCAULT

But Michael, it was in Foucault's intellectual company that you found a vantage point from which to reflect on and critique the cultural history of the psychotherapies and their very practices. Didn't this allow you to "think otherwise" than how you previously had "thought otherwise"? I say that because from the very first day I heard you speak about your work in 1981, I had no doubt that you "thought otherwise."[6] I recall standing up afterwards, as if being directed by some sort of compulsion, to announce to the attendees that they should be aware that they had witnessed "the founding of another school of family therapy." I was partly right because your life's work has turned out to be somewhat more than that. Prior to that, you had sought refuge in the political wing of family therapy in the 1970s, like I had.[7]

Michael, it was as if Foucault was directly addressing you at times, even if he was pretty opaque about it. Hadn't you already been discomforted in ways that I speculate Foucault had been discomforted when he worked in a psychiatric hospital as a psychology intern several decades before you did? Foucault provided you with a cultural history of ourselves, did he not? By

situating us within our own history and our own "therapy" culture, he provided you with the means and fortitude to not only
reflect on our practices but to reinvent them.

Foucault challenged the existing narratives about ourselves—
those that had us bringing the healing arts out of the darkness
and into the light of psychological expertise and their associated technologies. He informed us how new forms of power,
which he referred to as "expert power," became entangled in
new forms of knowledge. He, more than anyone I know, had
you look well beyond our benevolent intentions and take heed
of our effects: "We know what we think; we think we know what
we do; but do we know what we do does?" (Foucault, in Dreyfus & Rabinow, 1983, p. 187). Didn't you make it your mission
to track down those effects and when you found their source,
your small "p" politics was to seek remedies in your practice? In
your reading, Foucault went far beyond and outside an existing
critique of our practices. But by the same token, such a critique
brought you face to face with how we too are entangled in the
by-now established forms of "expert power" and the by-now
established forms of psychological knowledge.

Foucault had you consider "knowledge" away from any philo-
sophical sense of that. What he had done could be aptly called
"anthropologies of truth-making"; that is, how our "truths" come
to be produced and maintained. Where I believe your ethics
and politics came into play was with the invention of counter-
practices to those that authorized certain people to speak these
"truths" and excluded others from these "knowledges," thereby
organizing our world into *knowers* and those who appeal to such
knowledgeable persons. You saw to it that every one of your conversations in therapy was what you referred to as a "two-way
street," an exchange of reciprocal gifts.[8] Michael, you always
appeared to me to revere the other doubly: for their suffering
and for their *unsuffering* of themselves (King & Epston, 2009),
and for your conviction that they were possessed of "knowledges."

The philosopher John Caputo speculated on what kind of therapist Foucault might have been, given that he never expressed any explicit therapeutic intentions:

Such a therapy—if Foucault invented one that is—does not look at the mad as "patients" in the sense of objects of medical knowledge but as "patiens" —as ones who suffer greatly, who suffer from their knowledge. Such a "patiens" would not be an object of knowledge but an author or subject of knowledge, one from whom we have something to learn. (1993, p. 260)

Caputo went on to surmise that for Foucault as a therapist:

The healing gesture meant to heal this suffering is not intended to explain it away or fill in the abyss but simply to affirm that they are not alone, that we are all siblings in the same night of truth. The healing gesture is not to explain madness if that means to explain it away but to recognize it as a common fate, to affirm our community and solidarity. (p. 260)

Michael, compare this to my abstract of your version of solidarity:

And what of solidarity? I am thinking of a solidarity that is constructed by therapists who refuse to draw a sharp distinction between their lives and the lives of others, who refuse to marginalize those persons who seek help, by therapists who are constantly confronting the fact that if faced with the circumstances such that provide the context of troubles of others, they just might not be doing nearly as well themselves. (White, 1993, p. 132)

And didn't Foucault reveal to you the historical and cultural limits of these "expert" knowledges, not that it came as any surprise to you? It was my impression that Foucault confirmed your suspicions and gave you heart to persist with what you had already concerned yourself about in the institutions in which you worked during the 1970s and 1980s.

Did the Foucauldian vantage point give you some assurance that it might be possible to disengage yourself from the self-inspection, self-problematizing, self-monitoring, and confession by which we evaluate ourselves against "norms," according to which Nikolas Rose (1993) suggested our "souls are governed"? Why I ask is that you seemed to set great store in not doing what is expected of us, that we might "think otherwise" and expose those desires that had been "manufactured" in alignment with political, social, and institutional interests and refuse them.

It was against such reimagined social imaginary, Michael, that I watched those who had lost heart, time and time again, gain heart in their conversations with you. Through that means, they would appear to have breathed life into their own hopes for themselves and their futures. And most fascinating to me, they often found themselves to be invaluable and "respectworthy" (Lindemann Nelson, 2001), that is, worthy of their own respect and yours.[9]

Parallel with that, you made a great deal of trouble for problems, locating them in their cultural milieu, including the DSM technology and the pharmaceutical industry as two prominent sites of their construction. You "played" with problems instead of being haunted by them; you knocked them off the security of their perches by indicating that they are not beyond cultural analysis, as some of their advocates would have us believe.

John McLeod, the narrative scholar, justifiably regards narrative therapy as "postpsychological" and perhaps more aptly describes it as "cultural work":

In this respect, narrative therapy, therefore, can be viewed as a "postpsychological" form of practice (McLeod, 2004), or as a variety of "cultural work" (McLeod, 2005) rather than an application of psychological or medical science. Although narrative therapy retains some elements of the basic practice of "psychological therapies," such as talking about problems, consultation with a therapist, and so on, it largely by-passes psychological explanations and interventions, and instead seeks to help people by working with the ways in which they talk about issues, and the ways in which they participate in social life. (McLeod, 2006, p. 207; see also McLeod, 2004, 2005)

CONSIDERING TRANSLATION AND LITERARY GENRE

Michael, I am off on another tangent here, but I have been meaning to tell you that I have become interested in bilinguality (Sommer, 2003, 2004) and the politics of translation (see Epston, 2010; Polanco & Epston, 2009). I know whenever we talked about our books being translated into other languages, we would first marvel at the wonder of it, but then we would speak more soberly about our concerns around the export of knowledge. Would narrative therapy turn out to be like any other global brand? Or was it possible to "acculturate" narrative therapy practice to the culture, politics, and material circumstances of its recipients? If so, would these "border crossings" lead to mutation, if not transmogrification? By the way, *transmogrification* means to transform in a magical and surprising way. And could that be one of the means by which narrative therapy continually renews itself?

These questions led to a colleagueship with Marcela Polanco as she was beginning to translate *Maps of Narrative Practice* into Colombian Spanish. She was determined to "foreignize" rather than "domesticate" your text. As she engaged with this project, she was also constantly considering how your language was in some ways related to the literary traditions of Colombia, including magic realism.

Consider Marcela's comments on translating us both:

> I found a poetic resonance. It is not a language that tells about a lived experience; rather it is a language that once again brings the lived experience to life. It is like a living vocabulary. Life is happening in the vocabularies, not besides them or prior to them. When I was translating a story, I was living it. The idea of time that says that this story happened before and is now being told was irrelevant. (M. Polanco, personal communication, May 15, 2010)

And then compare this to our very first publication in 1985: "These questions are characterised by . . . a picturesque vocabulary drawn from the vernacular but at variance to everyday usage . . . a reconceptualization of time away from the restraints of linear 'clock time,' frequently involving the modification of tense" (Epston & White, 1985, p. 5).

Is it worth considering whether there is some connection between your narrative "style" and magical realism? Between your considerations of folk psychology (White, 2001) and "*sabiduria*"?[10] Would you be interested in reading a book entitled *Ordinary Enchantments: Magical Realism and the Remystification of Narrative* (Faris, 2004) with me? Would "ordinary enchantments" sit comfortably with you as a description of people's experiences of their consultations with you? These engagements with magical realism have led me to read South American writers, including the extraordinary Uruguayan writer, Eduardo Galeano (1992). He reminds me of you. If we miss you, we can read his stories. I think Galeano has solved a conundrum of yours and mine. Read on.

Do you remember how baffled you would become by workshop attendees accusing you of being unfeeling, often despite the fact you were visibly distressed in the interview? Remember how you would avoid the verb "to feel" because of its long association with expressive individualism (see Taylor, 2007, pp. 473–504), instead substituting such nouns as "expressions," "sentiments" and verbs such as "to experience." Well, Galeano provides an explanation in his "celebration of the marriage of heart and mind":

> Why does one write, if not to put one's pieces together? From the moment we enter school or church, education chops us into pieces: it teaches us to divorce soul from body and mind from heart. The fishermen of the Colombian coast must be learned doctors of ethics and morality, for they invented the word "senti-pensante," feeling-thinking, to define language that speaks the truth. (1992, p. 121)

We have to follow these leads, don't you think?

IMPROVISATION

Michael, you never cared to look over your genius, but I would like to consider your genius in improvisation. In your scintillating and respectful conversation with Salvador Minuchin at the Evolution of Psychotherapy Conference in 2005, Sal kindly insisted that there was so much more to your practice than the ideas on which you pinned it. You accepted this in principle by introducing the metaphor of jazz improvisation but locating that in the craft of musicianship. You insisted that that comes first. Could we take this metaphor seriously? And if so, aren't we going to have to consider pedagogies relevant to improvisation, once a person has mastery of their craft? Why don't we read Sudnow (2001), *Ways of the Hand: A Rewritten Account,* together? This is an autoethnography in which Sudnow pains-takingly describes how he becomes a jazz musician. And then why don't we talk to our friends who are engaged with narrative therapy and jazz.

Maps of Narrative Practice has no reference to improvisation, but I wholeheartedly agree with what you said: everyone has to first learn how to play and only then can they improvise. After all, I had always considered you to improvise within a structured framework of intention. And *Maps* provides such a plurality of remarkable frameworks of intention. Without this book to be read alongside *Maps*, were you ever concerned that "maps" might turn out to be "manuals" of the rules and regulations variety in which the spirit of this work could fade away?

RENEWAL

Good news, Michael! I know you will be delighted to learn that Stephen Madigan's book will be released any day (Madigan, in press). Stephen was like Boswell to your Dr. Johnson. He too has a hoard of audiotapes of conversations you had together from the early 1990s onwards. In the early chapters, he provides a history of ideas, the intellectual provenance for narrative therapy. You mention these references too in your posthumously published "Keeping the Faith" interview (Duvall & Young, 2009) and it is reassuring to me that this history has been recorded. Recalling those years puts me in mind of our wide reading in the social sciences during those intellectually tumultuous times.

Michael, I really want to consider if there is a danger of narrative therapy becoming theoretically passé. What do I mean by that? Surely Foucault was the most prescient commentator on the period from the end of World War II until 1980. But the world has changed so much over the last 30 years, has it not? Tony Judt writes:

> Something is profoundly wrong with the way we live today. For thirty years we have made a virtue out of the pursuit of material self-interest: indeed, this very pursuit now constitutes whatever remains of our sense of collective purpose. We know what things cost but have no idea what they are worth. We no longer ask of a judicial ruling or a legislative act: Is it good? Is it fair? Is it just? Is it right? Will it help bring about a better society or a better world? Those used to be political questions, even though they invited no easy answers. We must learn to pose them again. (2010a, p. 17; see also Judt, 2010b)

Don't you think that we in narrative therapy need to renew our reading of anthropology, cultural studies, sociology, women's studies, etc., to catch ourselves up to the world in which we live? That has always been narrative therapy's lifeblood. It was such fun for me in the 1980s, a scatterbrained sparrow pecking at seeds of ideas, to keep your mole company as you burrowed down into the world of ideas, digging your own tunnels through them until some years later they became distinguishably yours. In the same way, you marinated your preexisting practice with ideas until your practice became distinguishably yours. I remember to this day standing at the University of Auckland library reading Kevin Murray's paper "Life as fiction," which was a revelation to me, and of course its bibliography inexorably led us to Bruner and others (Murray, 1985; see also Epston, White, & Murray, 1992/1998).

I hope I have good news. It is too early to say. In such matters, time will tell. But I found a book chapter entitled "Stories Told and Lives Lived: An Overture" by Zygmunt Bauman (2001) and, despite my age, it has excited me in some ways similar to

reading Murray's paper in 1985. I have been reading Bauman
(2000), Sennett (2000), Ulrich Beck (1992), and most recently
Giddens (1992), and his "politics of living." These scholars are
trying to capture, both in theory and in life, the effects of the
new capitalism that has emerged in tandem with globalization.
I don't know yet where this will lead to, but if nothing else, it will
ensure that narrative therapy does not meet the fate of other
therapies that emerged at a specific place and in response to
their times. There is nothing sadder for me than a school of
therapy whose theory no longer is pertinent to current circumstances. And to top it off, yesterday I had one of those uncanny
experiences I love so much. I found a recent chapter by John
McLeod (2004) and read the following: "Narrative therapy creates a means of taking analysis of social problems offered by
sociologists such as Bauman (2004) and Giddens (1991), and
usefully employing these ideas within a therapeutic space" (p.
244).

How did he know that? Here is a quote from Bauman to whet
your appetite:

> Articulation is an activity in which we all, willy-nilly, are continu-
> ally engaged; no experience would be made into a story without
> it. At no time, does articulation carry stakes as huge as when it
> comes to the telling of the "whole life" story. What is at stake
> then is the acquittal (or not, as the case may be) of the awe-
> some responsibility placed on one's shoulders—and on one's
> private shoulders alone—by irresistible "individualization." In
> our "society of individuals" all the messes into which one can fall
> are proclaimed to have been boiled by the hapless failures who
> have fallen into it. For the good and the bad that fills one life
> a person has only himself or herself to thank or to blame. And
> the way the "whole-life story" is told raises this assumption to the
> rank of an axiom. (2001, p. 9)

Well, Michael, I agreed on a 5,000 word limit for this piece, and I expect I have exceeded that a bit. You know that bottle of Glenfiddich single malt whiskey I inherited from you? Well, believe it or not, there is just enough for two more glasses, one for you and one for me. Still, I wish you were here to drink for yourself.

NOTES

1. See a precedent for this in Epston, 1991/1998.

2. 8th International Narrative Therapy and Community Work Conference, Kristiansand, Norway, June 20–22, 2007.

3. "I want to speak of 'social imaginary' here, rather than social theory, because there are important differences between the two . . . I speak of 'imaginary' (i) because I'm talking about how ordinary people 'imagine' their social surroundings, and this is often not expressed in theoretical terms, it is carried in images, stories, legends, etc. But it is also the case that (ii) theory is often the possession of a small minority, whereas what is interesting in the social imaginary is that it is shared by large groups of people, if not the whole society. What leads to the third difference: (iii) the social imaginary is that common understanding which makes possible common practices, and a widely shared sense of legitimacy" (Taylor, 2007, p. 171).

4. The first published paper was White, 1984, reprinted in White, 1989b.

5. Compare Michael's 'experience of experience' questions in White, 1989c.

6. This was a workshop Michael presented at the 2nd Australian Family Therapy Conference in Adelaide, 1981; see White, 1989a.

7. One of the best accounts I have read of the spirit of these times in family therapy is Fraenkel, 2005.

8. "To accept without returning more is to face subordination, to become a client and subservient . . . while to receive something is to

receive a part of someone's spiritual essence. To keep this thing is dangerous, not only because it is illicit to do so, but also because it comes morally, physically and spiritually from a person. The thing given is not inert. It is alive and often personified, and strives to bring its original clan and homeland some equivalent to take its place" (Mauss, 1954, pp. 76–77).

9. In private correspondence, May 1, 2010, Hilde Nelson wrote: "To say someone is respectworthy is to say that they possess the greatest kind of value, not because they are useful for bringing about somebody else's goals or desires, but simple because they live a human life. They matter. They have dignity and so we owe them respect."

10. Marcela Polanco writes: "The word *sabiduria* translates into English as 'wisdom' or 'knowledgeablity'. *Sabiduria* is understood as a human virtue that develops through practical experience—it's the reason why elders are often considered as holding high levels of wisdom—and also by others' advice or example. Implicit in the meaning of *sabiduria* is a sense of the moral, which takes the wise person to make decisions based on a notion of justice. The origin of the word *sabiduria*, however, is not directly connected with the notion of holding knowledge about something, but to savour, taste, and enjoy it. This origin could make for yet another translation of *sabiduria* in English as 'knowledge savouring'" (M. Polanco, personal communication, June 6, 2010).

PART I

General Therapeutic Considerations

CHAPTER 1

Bringing the World into Therapy and Subverting the Operations of Modern Power

Of the many purposes that have shaped my explorations of therapeutic practices over the years, two are particularly relevant to my engagement with the narrative metaphor. One of these has to do with the imperative that I have placed on the development of therapeutic practices that decenter the voice of the therapist. Practices that decenter the voice of the therapist have the effect of bringing to the center of the therapeutic endeavor some of the "knowledges" of life and skills of living of the people who consult therapists. These are often knowledges and skills that are not very visible at the outset of therapeutic consultations. Amongst other things, the therapeutic practices that I am referring to here contribute to the rich description of these knowledges and skills that have been generated in the histories of people's lives, to elevating the significance of these, and to emphasizing the relevance of these to efforts to address the very problems and predicaments for which people are seeking help.

Another purpose that has been particularly relevant to my engagement with the narrative metaphor has been shaped by a commitment to deriving practices that are non-normative. Here, I refer to non-normative practices in the sense that they

do not, in an unquestioned and automatic way, simply reinforce and reproduce the valued forms of life of mainstream
culture—those ways of being in the world that are considered
to be "real," "appropriate," "healthy," and so on. I believe that
the narrative metaphor has provided fertile ground for this
project, which is one that has no end.

Throughout my engagement with the narrative metaphor,
I have taken care to emphasize, in text and through citation
in workshop presentations and addresses, that my explorations
are within a tradition of thought that is shaping inquiry across
a range of disciplines—from cultural anthropology to literary
theory, from ethnomethodology to discursive studies. And in
regard to explorations of the narrative metaphor within the
therapeutic disciplines, I have been aware that my engagement
with this metaphor is not unique. This metaphor has been taken
up by psychoanalysts in the reinterpretation of psychoanalysis
itself, by psychologists in the development of poststructuralist-
informed psychologies, and by other thinkers who locate themselves within the broad field of family therapy.

But even then, narrative analyses of the events of life are not
the special province of the professional disciplines. Narrative
analysis appears to be a primary, but not sole, cultural instrument for the making of meaning, one that is engaged quite routinely by people in their daily lives. People's engagement with
this instrument is most readily apparent when they are making
efforts to understand and to come to terms with that which
they find problematic in, or unsettling to, their lives. These
efforts are yet more prominent at those times when people are
seeking good listeners or soliciting advice within their familial/
friendship/acquaintanceship networks, and when consulting
counselors/therapists about their problems and predicaments.

For example, when people consult therapists, they frequently share their understandings of specific developments
in their own lives and in the lives of the people with whom

they are close by providing accounts of the unfolding of particular events of their world through recent history, and at times through more distant history. In providing this account, people also usually identify various themes that they associate with these events, and these themes often feature tragedy, loss, frustration, failure, and hopelessness. Further to these narrative understandings, people also routinely share with therapists their reflections on these events and themes, reflections that are often in the form of negative identity conclusions: "This tells us that he is out to destroy the family" (ascription of motive); "This shows how inadequate I am" (ascription of personal characteristic); "This will give you some idea of how pathetic I am" (ascription of trait); "This is proof of how needy I am" (ascription of disorder), and so on. These accounts of the unfolding developments of people's lives, the themes that are associated with them, and the identity conclusions that accompany these accounts often take the form of a problem-saturated narrative. Frequently this account is also represented by people as the dominant story of their lives.

Many, although by no means all, of the practices of what is often referred to as narrative therapy provide options for therapists to join with people in the "unpacking" of some of these dominant, problem-saturated stories of their lives. This unpacking has the effect of deconstructing many of the negative identity conclusions that are associated with these stories, and makes available to people other possible accounts of their identity, along with new options for action in the world. These therapeutic practices also provide options for therapists to join with people in the narrative analysis of some of the events of their lives that fall outside of these dominant stories—events of people's lives that are usually neglected in the sense that they are routinely passed over, without any conscious recognition of their potential significance. In the literature, this narrative analysis is often referred to as a "reauthoring" conversation. In these reauthoring conversations, people are invited to attach significance to some of these previously neglected events, and they are encouraged to link these together with other events of their lives in sequences that unfold through time according to alternative themes, or to what can be referred to as the "counter-plots" of their lives. As well, in this process, as people are invited by therapists to reflect on the events of these alternative themes or counter-plots, there is new opportunity for them to form identity descriptions that contradict the negative identity conclusions that are associated with what have been the more dominant stories of their lives.

There are various understandings about how these narrative-informed conversations lead to change. For example, there is an understanding that these contribute to people's lives becoming more evidently multistoried or more narratively resourced, and that this provides people with more options for meaning-making and for new possibilities for action in their lives. There is an understanding that the new identity conclusions that are generated in these conversations are embracing of people's lives, and that this contributes to possibilities for significantly different responses to the events of their lives. Then there are those understandings that point to the constitutive effects, or life-shaping effects, of the actual reauthoring conversations of narrative therapy. These understandings draw attention to the fact that, in these conversations, people engage in a performance of their lives, one that is significantly transporting of them—*transporting* in the sense that such a performance is an activity through which people become other than who they were at the outset of this engagement.

Although I continue to have a strong appreciation of the narrative metaphor, and expect that this will be an element that continues to shape my explorations of practice, this metaphor can never incorporate all of the considerations that are expressed in these explorations. For example, it cannot take us to considerations of a wide range of structures and cultural practices that, while they may be associated with particular narratives, cannot be reduced to, or accounted for solely through reference to, narrative analysis.

In regard to such structures and practices, I have always sought to address the diverse context of people's lives and to understand the specifics of how these contexts shape existence. This has contributed to a focus on familial contexts (whether this implicates family of origin and procreation, family of choice, or family of imposition), on many of the other institutions of society (including schools and workplaces), on material and social conditions of life (including economic disadvantage and inequitable social arrangements), on the power relations of local culture (including those of gender, race, class, heterosexism), and on the various elements of what is often referred to as discursive formations (including modern systems of understanding life and identity, customary ways of thinking and speaking about life and identity, the micro-practices of identity and of life associated with these, the rules for what counts as knowledge, for who may speak of it and under what circumstances it can be spoken of, and so on).

Despite the attention that I have consistently given, in my writing and in my teaching, to the significance of considerations of context in regard to life and to the development of practice, I often hear and read accounts of what it is that I am proposing that are quite reductive of this. Ironically, these accounts represent what it is that goes in the name of narrative therapy as reductive. For example, some have reached the conclusion that I have "proposed that life is nothing but a text," that I have "reduced reality to language," that I have "conflated narrative with discourse" (to the reduction of discourse), that I have "proposed an anything goes moral relativism," that I am "an anti-realist," that I have "reproduced the individualism and isolationism of contemporary Western culture by locating problems within individual meaning structures," and more.

I believe that some of these conclusions about the therapeutic practices that I have proposed are the outcome of identifying the body of these practices as a "narrative therapy." As this could well be an ongoing hazard, perhaps the description "narrative therapy" should be dispensed with, and other descriptions that draw attention to practices that address the contextual complexities of people's lives be established in its stead. But the narrative metaphor will continue to have relevance for me, as it is through stories that people are linked to culture. Stories about life and about identity are not radically constructed. They are not a stand-alone phenomenon, set apart from cultural discourses. Rather, stories of life and identity are shaped by the discourses of culture, and they are the bearers of these discourses. It is this appreciation of narrative as a cultural vehicle that is emphasized in many of the explorations of practice about which I have written and on which I have presented in a range of teaching venues.

This understanding of narrative as a cultural vehicle is featured in therapeutic conversations that unpack the stories of people's lives and identities. Not only does this unpacking contribute to the deconstruction of the negative identity conclusions associated with these stories, but it also renders more visible the modes of life and thought that are carried in these stories, the historical and cultural ways of being in the world and thinking about the world that these stories are the bearers of. These therapeutic practices bring the world into therapy in the sense that many routine and unquestioned understandings about life and ways of living become visible as cultural and historical products, and these are no longer accepted as certainties about life or truths about human nature and identity.

The understanding of narrative as a cultural vehicle is also featured in those narrative analyses that are usually referred to as reauthoring conversations. In these conversations, people do not radically construct alternative stories of their own lives and their identities. The alternative stories of life and identity that are derived in these contexts are of the pool of the discourses of culture, and they are also the bearers of ways of being in the world and thinking about the world that are cultural and historical. On account of this, these reauthoring conversations are not just about drawing out the alternative stories of people's lives, but also provide an opportunity for people to participate in the rich description of some of the skills of living and knowledges of life that are associated with the alternative stories of their lives and their identities. In narrative therapy, it is often assumed that the unique outcome or the exception provides the gateway or the point of entry to the alternative stories of people's lives. So too it is assumed that these alternative stories provide the gateway or point of entry to the exploration of other knowledges of life and of other skills of living or practices of life that are cultural and historical. In this way, it is not just deconstructing conversations that bring the world into therapy. Reauthoring conversations achieve this as well.

To give emphasis to this understanding of narrative as a cultural vehicle, and to give any priority to the significance of unpacking, in therapeutic conversations, the knowledges of life and the skills or practices of living that are associated with people's stories about life and identity, has the effect of foregrounding considerations of the particularly intimate relationship of knowledge and power. This particularly intimate relationship is the hallmark of a modern system of power that is the principal mechanism of social control in contemporary Western culture. In speaking of this particularly intimate relationship between knowledge and power, it is not my intention to contribute further to the familiar refrain that "knowledge is power," but to engage with a Foucauldian perspective on the mutual dependency of, on the one hand, the knowledges of

life and identity that have been produced in the human science
disciplines through the 300-year history of these disciplines,
and on the other hand, the practices of power that provide the
conditions of possibility for the employment of these knowledges in the constitution of, or in the fabrication of, modern
identities. It is through the development of these knowledges
of life and identity that the contemporary norms for life have
been constructed, and it is these practices of power that have
provided a technology for the disciplining of modern life in
the service of reproducing these norms. Together, these knowledges and practices come together in the normalizing judgment of people's lives. An analysis of modern power and the
operations of normalizing judgment is highly relevant to many
dimensions of therapeutic practice, as the following three stories demonstrate.

DIANNE

Dianne has been brought to see me by her parents, Joe and
Ellen, who are desperate about the state of their daughter's life.
They tell me that Dianne has experienced several admissions
to hospital over the past 18 months, a couple of which were
precipitated by suicide gestures, the others being the outcome
of their concerns for her general safety. In these admissions to
hospital, Dianne was treated for depression. Although Dianne
is cooperating with a course of medication that has been prescribed, Joe and Ellen tell me that they are concerned that they
can see little progress, and certainly nothing that is contributing to an abatement of their concerns about Dianne's predicament, and their predicament over not knowing how to be of
assistance to her. They tell me that, despite the hospitalizations
and the medication, Dianne is still withdrawn, expressionless,
disinterested, and "off the air" most of the time. In response to
this, they have become yet more worried about her, and they

are now on a search for what else might be done. Ellen is now crying, and Joe is attempting to soothe her. Dianne doesn't seem to notice—she appears to be away somewhere else in her mind.

I begin to ask Dianne some questions about whether she shares any of her parents' concerns about her own life, and if so, how she would define these concerns. Her minimal responses to my questions tell me little in any direct way, although in other ways, they also say a lot. These responses are perfunctory and guarded, and her expression remains wooden throughout this early part of our meeting. I have a sense that Dianne is shaping her responses so as to give nothing away, and so as to keep me at a distance. As I don't seem to be doing so well in my efforts to engage with Dianne, I decide to reflect on this and to ask Joe and Ellen if they have any ideas about what might be helpful in these efforts. They tell me that they don't think that they can do anything either, and that in my experience of Dianne's responses to my questions I am discovering just a little of what it is like for them in their efforts to get anywhere with their daughter. She doesn't seem to trust any efforts that anyone makes to get through to her. (I am not sure where to go next. I try opening my mouth in the hope that I will hear myself saying something wise, but to no avail. At this point, I find myself wishing that there were a therapist in the room.)

I turn to Dianne again. She briefly averts my gaze. I suddenly have an idea and can't figure out why it took so long in the coming. I say to Dianne that it is my guess that something is making it difficult for her to be present at this meeting and to join with us in this discussion about her life (I would like to say that in putting two and two together in this way that I am quick on the uptake, but this is hardly a very profound observation). I ask her if this is the case. No response. I say: "Well, it is my guess that there is something telling you not to trust me, which I suppose is pretty reasonable, since we have

only just met and you don't yet have a good measure of me."
Not a flicker from Dianne. "And," I say, "my guess is that you
have been through so much that it would be difficult to imagine that anyone else could understand." In response to this
speculation, it is my sense that Dianne has become yet more
stilled. Perhaps she is even holding her breath a little. This
encourages me. I say: "I guess that whatever it is that is telling
you not to trust me doesn't even want you to listen to what I
am saying, or even to give me the benefit of doubt in any way
at all." A flicker of expression on Dianne's face. "Well, if this is
the case, I would like you to know that I am used to these sort
of tactics." I now sense at least a minimal degree of engagement with Dianne. I ask a question of her: "Could it even be
that whatever is telling you not to trust me is also calling me
names?" Dianne registers surprise. "Do you know that this is
also something that happens to me a lot, and that I am used
to this as well?" Dianne quickly averts my gaze, which has the
effect of encouraging me further. "Yes, this is true," I say. "You
wouldn't believe the lengths that are gone to, and the names
that are used against me at times, in order to prevent people
from talking to me about what is happening for them. I think
it has a lot to do with jealousy and other things like this. Any-
how, I want to assure you that I am used to this and wouldn't
want you to be embarrassed by this."

I glance at Ellen and Joe and see that they are not sure what
to make of my statements. But they do seem interested in the
response that they are detecting from Dianne. I turn back to
Dianne and say: "Would you believe that I like to collect the
names that I am called? I compile lists of them. Some people
have stamp collections, and I have these collections of names
that I have been called. I think of this as my stamp collection
because these are names that I have been stamped with." Now
Dianne grins. So, I say: "I would like to go and get my most

recent list and read it to you. While I am reading this list, would you be prepared to listen to it, because I would like to know if there is anything else that you have heard about me, any other names that are not on this list, and that I might add to my collection?" Dianne grins again. "I would appreciate any offering. Believe me, none is too petty." I begin reading the list. Dianne is telling me that I had most of the ones that she is familiar with, and then seems happy to share with me two names that I can add to my collection. Now these specimens were particularly petty. Surely, I say, they could do better than this. Nonetheless I am gleeful about this opportunity to extend on my collection, and suddenly everyone in the room seems relieved.

This interlude provides a turning point in our conversation. Dianne begins to disclose the extent to which she is being tyrannized by very powerful and loud thoughts that she finds very difficult to resist. Amongst other things, these thoughts have set themselves up as an authority on other people's motives, and she doesn't know whom she can trust anymore. And these thoughts are constantly evaluating negatively everything she says and does, and demanding that she compare all of her actions and thoughts with the actions and thoughts that she would be having if she was a "real" individual—one who was properly together, one who was a person of substance—competent, confident, and independent. I learn that, in response to this constant experience of negative evaluation, Dianne is always redoubling her efforts to be a real person. But this never seems to work, and she mostly feels that there is nothing that she will ever be able to do that will make it possible for her to measure up. She is coming to believe that she will be forever totally inadequate—an extraordinary failure to be a person.

As our conversation proceeds, I find some opportunities to consult Dianne more fully about the operations of these powerful and loud thoughts. I ask her questions that encourage her to speculate about . . .

1. The nature of these operations (e.g., we talk about the tactics of power and control that are expressed in these operations and about the mechanisms of evaluation that are being employed);

2. What might be the general motivation and expectation behind the employment of these operations (e.g., we talk about how this has to do with a requirement for her to shape up, and for her to comply with an established program for her life); and

3. Those aspects that might provide us with a more particular account of the identity of these thoughts (e.g., we talk about what purposes these thoughts might have for Dianne's life, about what they might have dreamed up for her future, about what attitudes they routinely express toward her continuing efforts to have a life, about what they are invested in with regard to her current actions, and about what agenda they have for our meeting).

These explorations unpacked or deconstructed the loud and powerful thoughts that Dianne had found overwhelming. In this unpacking, the nature of these thoughts was becoming more known in its particularities. What had been intangible was now becoming relatively tangible. What had been experienced by Dianne as a total phenomenon was now appearing to her to be a phenomenon with limits and boundaries. The partial nature of what it was that had previously appeared to speak for the totality of Dianne's existence was becoming visible.

This exploration set the scene for the identification of various aspects of Dianne's life that appeared to stand outside the sphere of influence of these loud and powerful thoughts. These aspects included actions that couldn't be identified as self-evaluative, that couldn't be read as acts of comparison of one's self with what one should be. These aspects included expressions that could not have been shaped by the general motives and expectations associated with the operations of the loud and powerful thoughts. And these aspects included expressions of life that did not reproduce the particular purposes, dreams, and attitudes of these thoughts, but of other purposes, dreams, hopes, and attitudes.

At this point, we were presented with a number of options for our therapeutic conversation. There was the option of a conversation that might determine how it was that Dianne had in some ways refused what these operations of power were requiring of her in terms of self-evaluation and comparison: about the knowledges of life and skills of living that were expressed in this refusal, about the alternative ways of relating to her life and to the world that were evident in this refusal, ways that didn't measure up, that were not reproducing of being a "together" person—of self-possession, competence, confidence, and realness. Then there was the option of a conversation that identified the alternative purposes, dreams, hopes, and attitudes that were evident in the refusal of these operations of power, that traced the history of these in ways that contributed to them being more richly described, and in ways that linked these to the purposes, dreams, hopes, and attitudes of other people who had been significant to Dianne over the history of her life. Ellen and Joe made very significant contributions to this conversation. For example, in joining in the tracing of the history of these other purposes, dreams, hopes, and attitudes, Joe invoked the presence of his aunt, whose life he had always been fascinated with, who had always marched to the beat of a different drum despite the pressures on her to live life in more traditional ways. These and other options were taken up in subsequent conversations and provided a turning point in Dianne's life.

JENNY AND PAULINE

I am meeting with Jenny and Pauline. Pauline is providing me with some background information about what had led up to making the appointment to see me, and catching me up on the agenda that she and Jenny have for our meeting. In the process of doing this, Pauline talks of the loving relationship that she and Jenny have, which now has a 7-year history. Jenny is now joining Pauline in providing an account of what this relationship has meant to them both, and I ask some questions that provide me with an opportunity to gain a deeper appreciation of some of the special qualities of this relationship, and of what it has contributed to their lives and to their sense of who they are, to their sense of identity.

I learn that Pauline had called for the appointment, and that this had been with Jenny's blessing. Pauline tells me that although she knows that this relationship has brought many riches to both their lives, it has been a constant source of worry to her that Jenny gives herself such a hard time over so many things and frequently winds up in a state of despair, a state that is often hard to budge and that can leave them both feeling relatively paralyzed. Jenny verifies that this is the case and tells me that Pauline has been wonderful in her efforts to support her and to make her feel better at these times. Following a recent episode that had left Pauline feeling even more frustrated in her sense of being powerless to assist Jenny, she had proposed to Jenny that they make an appointment with me to explore other options for addressing this experience. Jenny had responded positively to this idea.

I ask Jenny if she has a name for this experience, and she says that "self-doubt" would be one that would fit quite well. This naming opens up the opportunity for an exploration of some of the specifics of Jenny's experience: We discover that self-doubt has Jenny treating herself harshly, that it saps her confidence, that it deprives her of a sense of well-being, and that it interferes in her relationship with Pauline and with other people who are especially significant to her.

In this exploration I find opportunity to consult both Pauline and Jenny about what they understand to be the context to the self-doubt: "In thinking about the nature of this self-doubt, do you have any sense that there might be particular forces that are in league with it, forces that might be shaping it and supporting it?" In response to this and other similar questions, Jenny and Pauline raise matters of sexual identity and homophobia, and of the structure and of the power relations of heterosexual dominance. Jenny also talks about certain experiences of growing up in her family of origin.

In this review of the forces that might be in league with self-doubt, both Jenny and Pauline inform me that although an understanding of these forces has been relevant to addressing a whole range of their experiences as lesbian women in a relationship with each other, and although they have a keen awareness of the extent to which these forces are still ever present in their lives, they have a sense that there is also somewhere else to look—that is, somewhere else apart from homophobia, the power relations of heterosexual dominance, and apart from identifying and working on family dynamics (which, by the way, had been exhausting them—*working* on things will do it every time). Pauline and Jenny tell me that they wouldn't want to lose this opportunity to turn over some yet unturned stones, that they see this as an opportunity for them to look beyond where they have previously looked. They also take time to assure me that they have developed some strong antidotes to these forces of homophobia and heterosexual dominance; for example, they have played a part in developing a strong and loving community of women who are there for each other in a multiplicity of ways in response to the effects of these forces on their respective lives.

In response to this proposal to look elsewhere, I ask Jenny and Pauline if it would be okay with them if I asked more questions about the effects of this self-doubt on Jenny's life and on their relationship with each other. This is acceptable, so I begin:

- "What does this self-doubt tell you about what sort of person you are?"
- "How does it shape your view of yourself as a person?"
- "What are the principal effects of this on your life and on your relationships?"
- "Could you catch me up on some of the particularities of how this self-doubt has you treating your own life?"

I learned that self-doubt was talking Jenny into the idea that she was inadequate as a person in this area or that, that she wasn't "enough this" or "enough that" (e.g., not individuated enough, not differentiated enough, and so on—you know, on the wrong end of the continuums and tables of life, on the "enmeshed" and "fused" ends, on the "blurred boundary" end of things—that she was a fraud, and that she was failing to be a real person). In short, Jenny spoke of a life that was marred by an array of personal lapses and omissions. In response to these conclusions, Jenny worked yet harder to be an adequate and together person, to shift her location in life to the preferred ends of these continuums so that she could become a real person, so that she could arrive at a place in which she was authentically who she really was, in which she was more completely who she could be. Jenny described these efforts as "hard work." Upon learning of the details of these personal gymnastics, it seemed to me that the description "hard work" had to rate as one of the understatements of the decade.

I now had a list of the lapses and omissions for which Jenny was giving herself a hard time, and I felt that I had a reasonable understanding of the conclusions that she was reaching in relation to these, and of the consequences of these conclusions in terms of how they affected her engagement with her life and her engagement in her relationship with Pauline. This list provided a basis for me to discern yet other expressions of Jenny's life that could also have been constructed as lapses or omissions, and for which, in a more ideal world, she could be giving herself a hard time over—lapses and omissions over which, in a more consummate existence, Jenny could be using as a basis for the generation of yet more negative conclusions about her identity. Indeed some of these omissions and lapses could have been taken up as a basis for the further verification of Jenny's concerns that she might be a failure to be a person.

"Would it be okay to have a conversation about these other expressions that could have been constructed as significant lapses and omissions in your life?" I asked.

Pauline responded, "I wouldn't miss it for the world"; Jenny said, "An opportunity that I couldn't possibly squander!"

"Well," I said, "could you help me understand how, in response to these potential lapses and omissions, you didn't insert yet other aspects of your life into a continuum of personal development or a table of performance? How were you able to refuse this? And, if these expressions of your life don't represent failure, what are they an expression of?"

Both Jenny and Pauline had considerable enthusiasm for this inquiry. It contributed to the rich description and honoring of their knowledges of life and skills of living; of alternative practices of the self that were nonevaluative; and of specific purposes, values, and beliefs that contradicted those purposes—values and beliefs that are embedded in the normative notions of what it means to be a real person in contemporary Western culture. Jenny broke from self-doubt.

DAMIEN

Damien was referred to me by the senior counselor of the agency for which he worked. At the time that he was hired, he was a young man who was generally considered to have great promise as a counselor. However, some 18 months down the track there is growing concern that this promise is not being realized. He is now considered to be indecisive, lacking in the assertiveness and self-possession that was expected of him in his capacity as a counselor in this agency, and as a role model for the volunteer staff who contributed significantly to the agency's service provision. The senior counselor was certain that his was just a "glitch" that could be quickly sorted out, a glitch that had diverted Damien from the path of a confident and full participation in the various contexts of agency life, a participation that would require him to assume some authority. It was considered that once this glitch was addressed, Damien would, without difficulty, be able to step into what was expected of him in these work contexts.

As I sit with Damien, he confirms this assessment of his performance. He says that he is at a loss to know what has derailed him. He recalls that, in the first place, when starting in this counseling position, he had experienced a degree of uncertainty that he assumed would soon dissolve as he learned the ropes and settled into the responsibilities associated with his position. However, it hadn't worked out this way. The uncertainty had snowballed, and now he found that at times he was virtually paralyzed by apprehension. This paralysis was creating a substantial predicament for him in relation to the work responsibilities that were expected of him. This had all weighed on him heavily, and he had followed up numerous avenues in his attempts to resolve this predicament, including assertiveness training. Alas, not only were these initiatives to no avail, but the outcome of them served to further complicate things: The failure of these efforts served to confirm the doubts that he had about himself and made him feel worse still.

From Damien's account of his experience in this workplace, I had a sense that some of his uncertainty and apprehension spoke to questions that he had about agency practice and about what was being required of him in his counseling practice. Because of this, I thought that it could be a good idea for us to unpack this apprehension so that we might have a clearer idea of the phenomenon that we were addressing. So, I asked Damien if it would be okay for me to ask some questions about this apprehension so that I might better understand its different aspects. I informed him of my purposes in proposing this. I said that while I understood some things about his experience of the negative effects of this apprehension, and could strongly appreciate his wish to be free of these effects, I thought that there might be yet more to this apprehension that it would be good to know about. He gave me the go-ahead. I asked: "Tell me, if it wasn't for this apprehension, would you be more or less modest in your conversations with the people who consult you?" In response to this question, Damien and I had a conversation in which he determined that immodesty, not modesty, would be more a feature of his work if it weren't for at least a degree of apprehension. We discussed some of the possible ramifications of this, which provided Damien with an opportunity to give some account of his preferred way of being with people, and to review what this said about his commitment to do what he could do to reduce the potential of power relations to do harm.

There was then a space in our conversations that allowed me to ask yet another question about Damien's apprehension:

"If this apprehension could be erased, how would its absence affect your ability to recognize and acknowledge the effects of what you say and do on the lives of the people who consult you?" In response to this question, Damien and I had a conversation in which he determined that such a development could shut the door on the option for him to take a degree of responsibility for the effects of what he says and does in the name of counseling. This led us into a conversation about the nature of his engagement with ethics and of the history of these ethics in his personal life.

Another question occurred to me: "If your practice was apprehension-free, whose knowledges would be more at the center of the conversations that you have with people who consult you? Your knowledges or the knowledges of these people?" Damien's response to the question was immediate: "It would be more likely that my knowledges were at the center." He then added that, for him, this would be a very unsatisfactory outcome, because it could contribute to the disqualification of highly relevant and significant knowledges that people bring with them into the counseling context. This led us into a conversation that identified Damien's position on practices that are sometimes entered into in the name of counseling and that have the effect of marginalizing the people who seek help.

Yet further questions occurred to me; for example, "In the absence of this apprehension, would you be more or less available to experience the contributions of the people who consult you, and the shaping influences of these contributions on your own life?" All of these questions contributed to conversations that unpacked Damien's apprehension and identified the aspects of this apprehension that might be valued, honored, and embraced. Our conversation then turned to an exploration of the possibilities that might be available for Damien to more openly and explicitly express his position on the power relations of therapy, on the ethics of practice, and on the values that challenge the marginalizing practices in his work with the people who consult him, and in his other work-related responsibilities.

Helen, the senior counselor of his agency, was then invited to join us for the third meeting. In the first part of this meeting, she was asked to be an audience to my conversation with Damien. This was a conversation in which his position on matters of power relations in therapy, on ethics, and on marginalizing practices was richly described, as were some of the knowledges and skills that been identified as available to Damien to take up in the expression of these positions in his counseling and other agency responsibilities. Then Damien sat back, and I had the opportunity to interview Helen about what she had heard in my conversation with Damien. As an outcome of this interview, Helen engaged in a retelling of what she had heard— a retelling that was powerfully acknowledging of Damien's position on these matters, and that richly described some of the knowledges and skills that he had identified.

As an outcome of this meeting, much of what was expressed in Damien's apprehension was valued, and Helen and Damien commenced a review of counseling and general agency practices in their organization.

MODERN POWER

What is common to these stories? I believe that the predicaments of Dianne, Jenny and Pauline, and Damien were very significantly the outcome of what could be defined as a technology of power. This is a technology of power that does not predominantly feature the mechanisms of prohibition, of oppression, restriction, and regulation that characterize the operation of traditional or classical structures of power. Rather, this is a technology of power that engages people in the fashioning of their own lives and of their own identities according to norms that have been constructed through the history of the modern professional disciplines. Rather than being prohibitive and restrictive, these technologies of modern power engage people in the production of their own lives through the disciplines of the self.

This technology of modern power can be considered "disciplinary" in two senses of this word. In the first sense, these power relations engage people in the fashioning of their own lives and in the fabrication of their own identities according to norms that have been constructed through the history of the modern "disciplines." And in the second sense, these modern power relations engage people in the production of their own lives through the "disciplines" of the self.

According to this account of power, the modern disciplines, including psychology, social work, and medicine/psychiatry, have been instrumental in the development of a disciplinary technology that routinely engages people in normalizing judgment of their own and each others' lives—judgment made according to norms about what a useful, productive, and authentic life would look like. These constructed norms, around which we are invited to measure our lives, are linked to our culture's truths of human nature; these truths of human nature are the favored identity categories of the modern era.

We are all incited to manage these truths by engaging in self-shaping activities that have the aim of closing the gap between our location on various continuums of development and tables of performance and the constructed norms that these continuums and tables are built around—so that we might become truly independent, autonomous, differentiated, and so on. It is the continuums of health and sickness, of normality and abnormality, and the tables that rank people in terms of whether they are backward or advanced in their performance that are the instruments of this modern power.

How many of you have not engaged in the comparison of

your lives against the constructed norms of our culture? Have not documented your position on this continuum or that? Have not entered your lives into this table or that?

It is in the context of these power relations that people are incited to reproduce the venerated individualities of contemporary Western culture. It is in the context of these power relations that people are recruited into acts in the management of the self by the self, into the reproduction of those ways of being that make available to them a small grant of normative worth in our communities—acts of self-enhancement, self-possession, self-containment, self-actualization, wholeness, and so on.

I have discussed just some aspects of modern power at work and have emphasized the role of normalizing judgment in this. To restate this point: *Normalizing judgment is the core activity of modern operations of power.* These operations of power are associated with the construction of knowledges of life and of identity that are assigned a truth status. These operations of power are generally effective in engaging people in an imperative to determine this truth, to reveal it, and to maintain faith with it in their acts of living. It is in this modern system of power that people's lives become objects of knowledge.

These operations of power "cellularize" life. The insertion of people's lives into these tables and continuums that are the instruments of normalizing judgment has a dispersive effect on groups of people; groups of people are supplanted by specific individuals who are dispersed and organized around a norm. In this way, this modern disciplinary power produces individuals.

Because the power relations of this modern system of power are everywhere to behold, opposition to these operations of power is everywhere to be seen. For example, this opposition is evident in some people's refusal to reproduce this culture's venerated individualities, which can be witnessed in what is often deemed to be their failure to achieve self-possession and self-containment, or their failure of any other criterion that informs this culture's account of personal authenticity. And opportunities to refuse these operations of power are ever-present. Take, for example, those opportunities that are available to people to resist the incitement to enter their lives into continuums of development, of health and normality, and those opportunities that are available to them to disengage from the practice of ranking their lives in this table or that table. And, in the context of this understanding of modern power, people's mistakes and errors, the unsettling contingencies of their lives, and at times even their misfortunes or failure to achieve desired ends can constitute unique outcomes.

Modern power is multicentered and multisited (rather than monolithic and total), and we are all implicated in the operations of this system of power as we go about fashioning our lives and our identities. This is a power that is everywhere. However, this is not a reason to despair. If modern power is everywhere to be perceived in its local operations, in our intimate lives and relationships, then there are endless opportunities available for us to develop an account of these operations, and to subvert them.

CHAPTER 2

Turning Points and the Significance of Personal and Community Ethics

In writing this chapter, I reflected on the turning points in the history of my practice. I was quickly overwhelmed by the flood of memories that enveloped my mind. There have been just so many of these. It would be impossible to ever do justice to all of the experiences that have contributed to these turning points. So, I have selected just a few of these experiences:

- Reflection and technical aids
- Inversions of concern
- Colleagues' voices
- The audience
- Personal and community ethics.

REFLECTION AND TECHNICAL AIDS

I will begin by addressing the part that technical aids have played in providing a foundation for some of these turning points. The tradition of recording interviews and reflecting on these recordings was part of what originally attracted me to the family therapy field. Over the years since that time, this tradition of openness and review has remained precious to me.

In the 1970s, I began to audiotape and videotape some of my interviews. Amongst other things, this technology provided me with the opportunity to experience some of the benefits of a hindsight that was not otherwise available to me (and, I might add, with the opportunity to experience considerable embarrassment). This is a practice that I have maintained over the years, and to this day I still look for the opportunity to listen to audiotapes and review videotapes of my conversations with the people who consult me.

It is through this listening and viewing that I have been able to distance myself from the immediacy of my experience of these therapeutic conversations, and to hear and see what I would not have otherwise been able to hear and see. This has undoubtedly contributed significantly to a number of turning points in my work.

Avenues for Conversation

What are these turning points? For a start, it is through these recordings that I have become more aware of a range of avenues for therapeutic conversations, and for the further development of particular avenues of conversation—avenues that were either not visible to me or of which I was not fully aware in the context of these conversations. On account of this, over the years I've experienced a broadening of my interest in people's lives, and an ever-deepening fascination with many of the thin traces of the neglected stories of their lives. This has inspired the development of narrative practices that contribute to an expansion of the panoramas of people's existence, panoramas that open to view many a tantalizing destination.

Listening to these recordings, and viewing them, keeps me in touch with my apprenticeship, which is one without end. This appreciation that there will always be avenues for rich story development that are not visible to me in the immediacy of therapeutic conversations means that I can never be wholly satisfied with my contribution to any therapeutic conversation. I find this inspiring, for it encourages me to put my mind to the ongoing development of the sort of therapeutic skills that might be of assistance in circumventing many of the cul-de-sacs with which we find ourselves confronted in therapeutic conversations—skills that might be of assistance in finding thoroughfares to rich story development.

Endurance of Initiatives

Second, it is through listening to and viewing these recordings that I became more aware of the multiplicity of initiatives that people routinely express in relation to the predicaments of their lives. It is one thing to know that people are not passive recipients of life forces. But it is another thing to identify these initiatives, and to contribute to a context that is favorable to their endurance. It is one thing to know that the totalizing and invariably pathologizing accounts of people's lives are social constructions that sponsor highly negative conclusions about their identities. But it is another thing to identify initiatives that might provide a point of entry to the sort of rich story development that brings with it more positive identity conclusions and new options for action in the world.

It is through the listening to and viewing of these recordings that I have become more aware of these options. This has been particularly important in circumstances in which there is a risk that I might totalize a person's identity—for example, the identity of a man who might be referred to me by the parole board for perpetrating abuse and who seems to champion abusive ways of being in the world.

It is partly through listening to and viewing these recordings that I have become aware of the fact that a good life is an outcome of 97% stalled initiatives, and that a troubled life is an outcome of 98% stalled initiatives. It is partly through this listening and viewing that I have reached the conclusion that therapeutic practice is successful if it plays a part in contributing to the endurance of 1% of the otherwise stalled initiatives of life.

Power Relations of Therapy

Third, it is through listening to and viewing these recordings that I have become more conscious of the power relations of therapy. There have been many ramifications of this, including the identification and naming of dishonesty in therapeutic practice.

An example: I had the opportunity to review a videotape of a recent therapeutic conversation with a 13-year-old young man and his mother and discovered that I had unwittingly paraphrased one of his mother's observations. This mother had observed that the workers of a high-security detention center had done good work with her son. In checking this conclusion with the son, I had paraphrased her statement in a way that had inverted this account: "Your mum has been telling me about how you did good work with the workers of this detention center. Does that fit for you?"

In this inversion, I had distorted the mother's words. Her words were clear enough, so, why would I do this? Perhaps this paraphrasing had to do with my hope that this young man might experience some degree of personal agency—the dominant account of his life was that he was incapable of directing the course of his life and incapable of predicting the consequences of his actions. He had been through significant trauma, and I am keenly aware of the consequences of such trauma to an individual's sense of personal agency. But whatever the impetus for this inversion, it was an expression of dishonesty and an implicit disqualification of this mother's voice—which, for a woman who has lived with significant disadvantage, must have been a replay of so many experiences of her life.

If I had wanted to bring forth an account of this young man's personal agency, I could have done so without manipulating his mother's words outside of her awareness and misrepresenting them to her son. For example, I could have asked questions such as these: "Your mum said that the workers of this detention center did good work with you. Did you respond to what they had to offer, or did this bounce off you? Did you take some of this in, or did you reject this? And if you did take some of this in, how did you open yourself to this?"

In this acknowledgment of dishonesty, I am not diminishing my work, and I am not putting myself down. It is because I love my work that I am highly motivated to identify any abuses of power and to root them out. I believe that if one is not tripping across abuses of power in one's therapeutic practice, it means that one has gone to sleep. Listening to and viewing recordings of our work can provide us with an avenue to identify abuses of power within the context of the therapeutic relationship.

INVERSIONS OF CONCERN

The second theme I wish to consider involves inversions of concern. Consider this example.

I had known Donna for several years. She was first brought to see me by her parents, who were very concerned about her quality of life. Donna had a diagnosis of schizophrenia, had been on medication for several years, and had experienced a number of admissions to a psychiatric hospital. She rarely ventured outside of the family home, and on the occasions that she did so, it was always in the company of a family member, and with great fear and trepidation. I had a series of meetings with Donna and her family over a period of 8 months, and during this time she began to step into the world and to develop a life for herself—in fact, she became quite adventurous. She would still visit me occasionally for what she referred to as a "top-up." This was usually at times when she was experiencing stress in regard to a new step that she had taken or was proposing to take, or when she was going through a crisis of one sort or another.

On this occasion of meeting with Donna, I hadn't seen her for 5 months. At the end of our conversation, she looked around my interviewing room, took in the surroundings with a studied eye, and exclaimed: "What a mess!" She was mostly referring to my filing system—at the time I had a horizontal filing system and could never find what I was looking for. My response: "Yes, it really is a mess. And I am determined to do something about this." Donna's response: "What makes you think that you are ready to take this step?" There was something ever so familiar about this question. I laughed, and did my best to respond. Then, a further question from Donna: "I guess this decision didn't come out of the blue. What led up to it?" Now we were both laughing. Donna continued to scaffold this interview with questions like: "When do you think that you will be ready to take this step?" "Sometime in the next week or two, I guess," I said.

We chatted some more, and I then accompanied Donna down to the reception area. There, to my surprise, Donna made another appointment to meet with me, this time in 2 weeks. I remarked that this was a departure from her habit of leaving it until she felt that she needed another top-up. "Oh," Donna responded enthusiastically, "This appointment is not for me, it's for you! I have made a time for you to see me in 2 weeks to see how you went with this plan to fix up your mess." I was open-mouthed.

Donna had made the appointment time for early on a Thursday morning, and I was up half the night on Wednesday getting my filing system into a vertical format. I then managed a few hours sleep, before fortifying myself with caffeine ahead of my meeting with Donna. It was a fantastic event. Donna dramatically swept into my room ahead of me and loudly proclaimed: "What a change! You really got it together!" Then she paused:

"But I shouldn't say that. It is what you think of this that counts."
We were again laughing together, with Donna making it even
more difficult for me to collect myself by asking questions like,
"How does this affect your picture of yourself?"

It is experiences such as this one that have been a powerful
antidote to any conception that I might have held about one-
way accounts of the therapeutic process. These experiences
have rendered more visible people's contribution to good therapeutic conversations and to good therapeutic outcomes. Such
experiences have rendered more visible the extent to which, in
these therapeutic conversations, we are joined by the people
consulting us, the extent to which we are encouraged by them
when these conversations are on track, and the extent to which
they are patient with us when things are off the track. Such
experiences have rendered visible, to me, the extent to which
many of the people who consult us persevere with us through
thick and thin.

And it is also experiences like this one that emphasize the
extent to which the people who consult us include us in their
lives. It is these acts of inclusion that inspire my efforts to identify the ways in which therapeutic conversations are touching
my life, and to find appropriate, ethical ways of acknowledging
this in the context of these conversations. This act of acknowledgment is clearly significant to the people who consult us, but
it is also significant to our lives as therapists. For these acts of
acknowledgment contribute to the endurance of initiatives in
our own lives and work that might otherwise be stalled.

COLLEAGUES' VOICES

Throughout the history of my practice, the voices of colleagues
have also contributed to significant turning points. Here I shall
offer two examples.

The time is the 1980s. I am away from Adelaide presenting

a workshop on working with couples. Ahead of my teaching I have the opportunity to catch up with some friends and colleagues whom I'd not seen for while.

I have now started the workshop and I am about a half an hour into my teaching. Suddenly, one of my colleagues stands up and says, "I can't hear you, Michael." I respond with: "Sorry, I'll turn up the sound." This colleague says: "Michael, that's not it. It is that when you talk about your work with couples, and you mean heterosexual couples, then you render my relationship with my partner invisible, and you also render my identity as a lesbian invisible. So, it would make it a lot more possible for me to hear you in a presentation on couples who are heterosexual if you were to say "heterosexual couples."

This was a challenge to my unwitting expression of heterosexual dominance, an expression that violated my own value system and the position that I hold on questioning the power relations of local culture. This challenge contributed to another turning point in my understanding of expressions of heterosexual dominance. Since this time I have been more aware of the pervasiveness of heterosexual dominance, of its multiplicity of forms, of the potential for me to inadvertently reproduce this in the name of therapeutic practice, and of the extent to which heterosexual dominance is directly implicated in the predicaments of people's lives, including many young people who find themselves evicted from their homes and who might be suicidal.

It has become fashionable for some to read my reference to heterosexual couples when talking about my work with couples, and to gay or lesbian couples when I am talking about my work with gay/lesbian couples, as an example of my efforts to be "politically correct," with a negative meaning associated with this. However, it is my sense that I am honoring what people who are in subject positions say about what words mean to them, and about the politics associated with unquestioned discursive practices.

A second example of the significance of colleagues' voices occurred some years ago when I was invited to provide consultation to an organization that was set up by Aboriginal people to provide services in regard to violence in Aboriginal families. In response to this invitation I found myself struggling with significant dilemmas. I am a member of the white culture, and it is the policies and actions of my people that have been so detrimental to Aboriginal culture throughout the history of the occupation of this country. Amongst other things, this occupation has been achieved through the dispossession of a great number of Aboriginal children from their families, and through this, the dispossession of parenting skills. And as a man of white Australian culture, I am of the group that has been primarily responsible for these policies, and for ordering them. My dilemma: I could perceive a direct line between what I was being consulted about and my existence here in this land.

I struggled with this dilemma for some weeks in my early consultations with the people of this agency. Then, in a conversation with the director of this service, I named this dilemma and talked of my struggle with it. Her response was kind but confronting: "Do you think that it is okay for you to own this dilemma, to simply assume that it is just yours to have, to simply assume that it is just up to you to go off and sort this out? This is typical of many of you whites. It is about privilege. It is about assuming that you are entitled to independently come to some resolution of this. But these considerations affect all of us. Don't think that we haven't considered this dilemma from the other side. But it is not so simple for us. If we don't proceed in the development of this service, then our people suffer. So, this is a shared dilemma that we can talk about together. We will all share this dilemma, and it will be clear to you when it is time to go."

This challenge contributed to another turning point in my understanding of expressions of white privilege and of the mechanisms of these expressions. Since this time I have become more conscious of what constitutes expressions of white privilege, and, in my work in partnership with Aboriginal colleagues, I have taken the opportunity to become more fully acquainted with the consequences of these expressions.

THE AUDIENCE

The fourth theme I wish to describe in relation to the turning points in my work relates to the considerations of the audience.

David Epston and I have a long history of engaging audiences to the preferred developments of people's lives. In the latter part of the 1980s, after becoming acquainted with the work of cultural anthropologist Barbara Myerhoff, we began to conceive of the people we recruited to this role as outsider-witnesses. This was a very significant development in our work.

What was the genesis of this? I recently had the opportunity to view some old videotapes of my therapeutic conversations with young children and their families. One of the things that stood out was the extent to which these young children were routinely engaging an audience to the new claims about their lives that were generated within the therapeutic context. Some were taking their certificates of progress and achievement to school to share with peers, and others were demonstrating, often in dramatic fashion, their newfound competence to their siblings and cousins. It was clear that these audiences were playing a significant role in the authentication of these new claims and in furthering the preferred plots of these children's lives. Though not fully conscious of the significance of the audience to the changes in the lives of the children with whom I was meeting, in hindsight I have no doubt that these experiences provided a significant part of the inspiration for subsequent developments in my active recruitment of audiences.

Over the last decade or so, my explorations of the outsider-witness contribution to the authentication of alternative identity claims have led me to develop a therapeutic "map" to guide outsider-witness responses. It is not my intention to outline this development here. Rather, I will tell a story about my contact with a boy called Nathan whom I met some 20 years ago. I have chosen to tell this story because it represents one of a number of experiences that contributed to my conviction that the appropriate outsider-witness can achieve what I cannot achieve as a therapist. It was experiences like this that encouraged me to engage in further explorations of the sort of therapeutic inquiry that decenters the therapist.

Nathan had been in lots of trouble in virtually every aspect of his life—with school authorities, with the police, with the parents of his friends, and with his own parents. In the context of my work with him and his family, and in the context of rich story development, Nathan gave voice to the claim that he was "making a comeback" from trouble. I was curious about this "comeback" metaphor and inquired about the history of his familiarity with it. In response I learned that this familiarity was the outcome of his participation in little athletics—he was familiar with the notion of an athlete's comeback from injury. At this time, Nathan's parents also informed me that he had been expelled from little athletics on account of his "bad behavior."

It occurred to me that an athlete who'd made a recovery from injury would be an ideal outsider-witness to Nathan's claim to be making a comeback. I had a sense that an appropriate response from such an outsider-witness would contribute to Nathan's feeling more at one with this claim, and that this would shape his actions. I happened to know a triathlete who'd performed quite well on the local scene and who'd made a comeback from injury. I wondered aloud whether Nathan would be interested in meeting with this athlete over the subject of comebacks, over

what goes into the preparation for these, over the potential set-
backs to be faced and endured, and over the determination
required to see them through.

Nathan and his parents were enthusiastic about this idea, so
I said that I would see what could be arranged. I contacted the
triathlete, whose name was Rod, filled him in on what I had
gained permission to share with him, and asked if he would
be prepared to meet with Nathan. Rod said that he would be
prepared to do whatever he could to be helpful within the time
constraints that he was presently managing. He suggested that
Nathan come to the athletics track on the coming Thursday
evening at 5:30 P.M., and at this time he would put aside 20
minutes or so to talk with Nathan about the subject of comebacks. I asked Rod to leave it to Nathan to raise anything that
he wanted about the comeback that he was embarking upon.
Rod said that he understood, and that he wouldn't ask any
intrusive questions.

The meeting duly took place. The parents waited in the car
park not for 20 minutes, but for an hour and 20 minutes! On
several occasions they became concerned about what Nathan
might be up to—was he graffitiing the stadium walls or caus-
ing some other form of trouble? However, upon checking they
found Rod and Nathan in earnest conversation. Eventually,
Nathan came sauntering across the car park and nonchalantly
slid into the back seat of the car. "What happened?," asked
the parents. "Oh, we were just having a man-to-man conversation," replied Nathan. The parents then learned that, in the
context of this conversation about the nature of comebacks,
and the trials and tribulations associated with them, Rod had
told Nathan that when he was Nathan's age he was also in a
lot of trouble and that his life was going down the drain. Rod
had talked about the decision that he'd made about making a
comeback from trouble, and about the difficulties he'd experienced in following through with this decision. However, he'd

persevered and eventually succeeded. Rod then remarked that if he hadn't had this experience of making this comeback from trouble under his belt, then he probably would not have been able to persevere in his comeback from injury—instead, he would have given up. Apparently, on several occasions during the conversation, Rod had said: "So, all of the trouble that I went through was not for nothing."

As he and his parents pulled up at the family home, Nathan exclaimed, "You know, my life was going down the drain too, but it hasn't been all for nothing!!" From this point on, there was no turning back for Nathan. Although he too experienced ups and downs over the course of his comeback, he never wavered in his determination to make it. And it was very clear to me that Rod had achieved something in relation to Nathan that I couldn't achieve as the therapist.

It was the realization that, in many circumstances, the outsider-witness has the potential to achieve something that is beyond the therapist that encouraged me to prioritize explorations of outsider-witness practices in the context of therapeutic conversations.

PERSONAL AND COMMUNITY ETHICS

I have given several examples of experiences that have contributed to turning points in the development of my work. These related to the listening and viewing of recordings, to the voices of the people who consult me, to the voices of my colleagues, and to the voices of outsider-witnesses to my therapeutic conversations. Amongst other things, it has been experiences like these that have provided me with the opportunity to identify abuses of power within the therapeutic relationship, to develop a stronger consciousness of the power relations of heterosexual dominance and of expressions of white privilege, to recognize the contributions of the people who consult me, and to acknowledge that outsider-witnesses can often achieve something that I, as a therapist, cannot.

Opportunities like these don't just present themselves to us. We respond to them. What is it that shapes the sort of responses that I have described in this chapter? Of course, I am familiar with some of the unkind answers to this question—answers that diminish and demean such responses by representing them as founded on forms of "purism" and "political correctness." But I have no interest whatsoever in what is sometimes referred to as "purism," and I have not endeavored to be "politically correct." However, I have been interested in the sort of personal and community ethics that encourage me to honor what people say about the consequences of:

- Abuses of power within the therapeutic relationship
- The reproduction of the power relations of local culture, including those of heterosexual dominance
- Expressions of white dominance and the forms of these expressions
- The acknowledgment of the contribution of the people who seek consultation
- The contribution of outsider-witnesses and the importance of decentering the therapist through privileging the macro-world of life over the micro-world of therapy.

It is these personal and community ethics that have shaped my responses to the experiences I have discussed in this chapter. It is through these personal and community ethics that these experiences have constituted turning points. These are the sort of personal and community ethics that emphasize our responsibility for the consequences of what we say and do in the name of therapeutic practice; that encourage us to introduce structures that make us more accountable to the people who consult us; that encourage us to acknowledge that the people in the subject position in the power relations of our culture know a lot more about our habits of thought and action than we do; that underscore the phenomenon of a relational self rather than the phenomenon of the encapsulated self that is the vogue of contemporary Western culture; and that encourage us to question the extent to which we might be accomplices to the operations of both traditional power and modern power.

The experiences that I have described in this chapter constituted turning points because they offered me the opportunity to bring my practice more into harmony with the sort of personal and community ethics that I take as my principal guide to practice. But this assertion about the priority of considerations of personal and community ethics conflicts with two assertions that presently hold sway in the culture of therapy/counseling. One of these is the assertion given to the priority of evidence and to the central validity of notions regarding evidence-based treatments. According to this assertion, any approach that is evidence-based is given an overriding status.

The second of these contemporary assertions concerns the primacy of the therapeutic relationship. This assertion argues that it is exclusively the therapeutic relationship that is relevant to therapeutic outcome, and that this is common to all of the therapies, regardless of persuasion or orientation. According to this assertion, most therapies are more similar than distinct in this regard, and therapeutic persuasion and orientation matter very little.

However, it seems to me that the assertion that we must have evidence and that the therapeutic relationship is important is to say very little at all. I don't think anyone would doubt that evidence is important to outcome, and I don't think anyone would doubt the significance of the therapeutic relationship to outcome. But the question is, what sort of outcomes are we talking about? I think that it is this question that brings to the foreground matters of personal and community ethics. It is this question that renders personal and community ethics critical to any consideration of therapeutic practice.

Just one example to clarify the position that I am taking here: I recently read an account of therapeutic practice in which a man who was struggling with some issues around anxiety was judged to be lacking in appropriate assertiveness. Examples given of this lack included the fact that although he gets annoyed when others cut in on him whilst driving, he doesn't give expression to this in the usual way—that is, he doesn't make a big thing out of it. An evidence-based therapeutic approach was employed, and the therapist gave considerable priority to the development of the therapeutic relationship. As an outcome of this therapeutic approach, this man stepped into a stronger sense of entitlement in circumstances like the one that I have outlined, and as a result was able to give expression to his frustrations in life by responding "more appropriately"—that is, by making a bigger deal out of these frustrations. Of course, there is evidence that the approach worked, and I have no doubt whatsoever that the therapeutic relationship was a highly significant factor in this outcome.

Now, let's reimagine this work. Imagine that you are meeting with the same man who is struggling with some issues around anxiety. And imagine that you also hear some of these stories about this man's experiences of the world, including the story about driving frustrations. And in response to this, you find yourself curious about how it is that this man was able to avoid expressing a sense of entitlement in relation to these frustrations, about how he avoided making a big deal out of these types of situations. Now imagine that this curiosity contributes to this man becoming interested in, and then fascinated with, this sentiment of living that doesn't reproduce that which is venerated in men's culture, and in the history of this sentiment of living in his life. And imagine that in the context of this conversation this sentiment of living becomes more richly known, and that this man becomes more familiar with some of the knowledges of life and skills of living associated with this sentiment. Imagine that as an outcome of this exploration, he finds that he is able to respond more flexibly to a range of predicaments, experiences pride in relation to the position he has taken on many taken-for-granted ideas about life and identity, and finds himself in a more harmonious place in life. Now, of course, as with the first scenario, there is evidence that the approach worked, and there is no doubt that the therapeutic relationship was a highly significant factor in this outcome as well. Thus, to assert that evidence is important and that the therapeutic relationship is a highly significant factor is to say very little at all.

Is it our role to be the unwitting accomplices of modern power, or is it our role to sponsor diversity in everyday life? Is it our role to promote single-storied conceptions of life—or to bring forth complexity in the sense of alternative stories of life? Is the therapy room a context for the confirmation of the known and familiar, or is it a context for arriving at what it might be possible to know? Is it a context for domesticating the exotic, or is it a context for "exoticizing" the domestic?

CONCLUSION

In this chapter, I have outlined a number of experiences that have contributed to turning points in the history of my practice. Furthermore, I have described how my responses to these experiences were shaped by particular personal and community ethics. To conclude, I believe that progress in the development of our work hinges on the priority that we accord to personal and community ethics. Without according priority to these considerations we are vulnerable to becoming oblivious to diverse acts of life, and to the significance of acknowledging this diversity. Without according priority to these considerations, we are vulnerable to the sponsorship of the taken-for-granted discourses of our culture that foster lifestyle conformity. Without according a priority to these considerations, we are vulnerable to becoming unwitting accomplices to the operations of traditional power in the reproduction of inequality, and to the operations of modern power in the reproduction of the venerated norms of our culture.

CHAPTER 3

Power, Psychotherapy, and New Possibilities for Dissent

It is commonly assumed that the therapeutic context is sacrosanct. This assumption makes it possible for therapists to treat the therapeutic context as if it were exempt from the structures and the ideologies of the dominant culture, and it guarantees the unwitting reproduction of this culture. In the process of any therapeutic interaction that is guided by this assumption, it is likely that the very aspects of ideology and social order that provide the context for the problems that people experience will be reinforced (e.g., the veneration of rugged individualism and the reinforcement of oppressive gender roles).

In this chapter, I discuss examples of the reproduction of dominant culture in therapy—in terms of the structure of the therapeutic context and in terms of the knowledges that are deployed in this context—and I review the real effects of this reproduction on the lives of all parties to therapeutic interaction. I also discuss certain implications of this analysis—implications that require us to revision the therapeutic context, that lead to the dismantling of some of the accepted structures and practices of therapy, and that point to the creation of contexts that open new possibilities for dissent.

POWER AND THE CULTURE OF THERAPY

In recent years, many therapists have been struggling with the same issue: how to change the culture of therapy. Revisioning therapeutic practices is not an easy thing to achieve, but we can find ways to do this. If the culture of psychotherapy has played a central role in the reproduction of this culture, then it can also play a central role in dismantling it. A very great number of us are playing a significant role in the development of processes and structures that are contributing to important transformations in relation to power and the culture of therapy. This is the context within which this chapter is written.

James

James introduces himself as a "schizophrenic." He tells me of his history of psychotic episodes and of his hospitalizations. He gives me details of his principal diagnoses and of his various medications. He then begins to reflect on the general state of affairs in his life and in the process introduces me to the deep sense of despair that he struggles with on a day-to-day basis. He tries so desperately hard, and yet every time he comes undone. He so much wants his life to go forward, yet time and again, what he calls "episodes of the voices" shatter the headway.

I ask what *going forward* means to him. For a while he searches for words. Then tears fill his eyes. James says that he feels like a failure. He says that *going forward* means so many things. It means being able to be virtually everything that he is not. It means being a real person. It means not being dependent. It means being able to stand on his own two feet, being able to reassure himself. It means being appropriately assertive. It means being a together person. And, perhaps, above all other considerations, it means being acceptable. James had tried so hard to be acceptable in the eyes of others, to receive his grant of moral worth in the eyes of a community of persons of which he skirts the periphery.

James is telling me that at times he has developed some fairly grand ideas about who he might be, and some grand plans. But all of these have come unstuck. I find myself musing. Delusional? Maybe. But "bravado" might be a better word for this. James wants to know if I think there is any hope for him. Can I do anything to help him to feel okay about himself, to help him become a person?

Jenny

Jenny briefly introduces herself and then informs me that she has been quite depressed recently, and desperate as well. Thoughts of suicide have not strayed far from her mind over the past 3 months. She is now very worried that she might follow through on these thoughts. She doesn't think that she could feel more worthless than she does right now. Her face is expressionless. No, actually not expressionless, but it features a ghostly resignation.

I ask, "Do you have any idea of how you were recruited into this sense of worthlessness?" She does. Jenny tells me something of the traumatic circumstances of her childhood, of her adolescence and early adult life. But she thought that she had got through all of this and had somehow reached some resolution of it all. She'd worked hard enough at it. And life had been going better for her. Now, however, with the resurfacing of the depression without rhyme or reason, she felt that all of the work that she had put into this had been for nothing, and that she was back to square one. She felt at the mercy of this depression. She had virtually given up.

Suddenly, I hear myself saying that in my experience, depression doesn't just come out of the blue. Could I ask some questions about recent events? Yes, this would be okay. I am learning that Jenny first experienced a renewal of the depression while away on holiday, approximately 3 months before our meeting. She had taken this unexpected descent into depression as a confirmation of her worthlessness, for it suggested to her that work was just a way of avoiding her inadequacy and escaping her nature, which she now assumed to be basically depressive.

Upon inquiring further about the events associated with this holiday, I learned that Jenny had taken the opportunity to catch up on some reading. What sort of reading, I asked. Now get this: It was three popular psychology books that had been prescribed by a counselor, two on the subject of "authenticity," and one with the title *Women Who Love Too Much*!

Sally's Family

Sally, in her mid-20s , is accompanied by her parents, Janet and Steve, and by her brother, Scott, and her sister, Helen. Sally has a history of anorexia nervosa that now stretches over some years. She has been subject to various treatments, including periods of hospitalization.

After introductions, family members fill me in on the details that they believe important for me to know. I then ask what understandings they have gathered about anorexia nervosa in their consultations, and which of these understandings make the most sense to them. In response to this question, I am about to witness the performance of a familiar story. Sally, already sitting at the periphery of the family group, turns her head to look at the wall. I then notice that there are tears streaming down Janet's face. Janet responds to my acknowledgment of this by telling me that at least she now has "insight" into the problem. What sort of insight, I ask. Janet says that she has realized that the problem has a lot to do with her. She has been too close to her daughter, certainly overprotective and perhaps controlling of her. Janet is now sobbing, and Sally appears even more remote, which I hadn't thought possible. Other family members don't appear to know what to do, even where to look.

Soon I am asking family members what ideas they have learned, in their various consultations, about the solution to the problem. I have the sense that I am about to hear another very familiar story. Steve is telling me that Sally has to learn to be more independent. Janet has recovered somewhat and also contributes. She says that the solution is for Sally to individuate and to disengage herself from her relationship with her mother, and from the family more generally.

Power and Psychotherapy: The Neglected Dimension

When it is assumed that the therapeutic context is exempt from the structures and the ideology of the dominant culture, this encourages therapists to proceed with their work in a manner that is characterized by a certain vanity, a manner that is informed by a strong sense of security. This vanity is such that it even informs discussions and debates by therapists about whether or not they should bring considerations of the politics of relationship into therapy, or even whether or not the politics of relationship are relevant to therapy.

At times I have even been asked to join debates about whether or not it is the therapist's place to bring politics to therapy. My standard response to such invitations is that, according to its terms, the debate is irrelevant and presumes a certain arrogance; that it is never a matter of whether or not we bring politics into the therapy room, but whether or not we are *prepared to acknowledge* the existence of these politics, and the degree to which we are prepared to be complicit in the reproduction of these politics. How could the therapeutic context possibly be exempt from the politics of gender, race, and class? How can therapy be exempt from the politics associated with the hierarchies of knowledge and the politics of marginalization in this culture? When people walk into the therapy room, they bring with them the politics of their relationships. And when people walk into a therapy room, they walk into a context that is structured by politics.

Even a cursory examination of the above vignettes so clearly demonstrates that the assumption that therapy has some privileged location outside of the culture at large cannot be sustained. What happens to our options for therapeutic action when we consider James's experience of being a spectacular failure as a person in the light of this culture's veneration of rugged individualism, one that specifies self-possession and self-containment? How might the course of therapy be affected by an acknowledgment of the extent to which this specification of personhood excludes him from the grant of moral worth that is allocated to persons in this culture who have more success in reproducing this specification? We can perceive the negative effects of the stress and personal distress that James experiences in his life, but what are the implications for our therapeutic interactions when we appreciate these negative effects as the outcome of the extraordinary stress that James subjects himself to in his efforts to receive this grant of moral worth? In the light of these questions, how are we going to relate to his plea to assist him to become a real person?

And what about Sally's experience? How might our work proceed if we were to review her experience in the light of modern systems of power that recruit persons into the ongoing evaluation, judgment, and policing of their own lives? What difference might it make to our interaction with Sally if such an appreciation of the context of her depression turned out to be relevant? What alternative courses of action might be available to Sally if the extent to which she was being incited to tyrannize herself into a state of authenticity became apparent—if the ruse was exposed through some determination of the ways of life and ways of thinking that stand in the shadows of this word *authenticity*? And how might we prioritize the context of gender politics if we took the opportunity to explore which ways of being in the world were being championed by titles like *Women Who Love Too Much,* and which ways of being were marginalized and disqualified in the process? What might happen if the therapist were to ask Sally whether she has ever heard of a book titled *Loving Women in Relationships with Men Who Don't Love Enough*? Is it possible for women to love too much when this love is reciprocated?

What happens to our orientation in this work when we are able to entertain and to explore the possibility that the symptoms of anorexia nervosa are by-products of the misogyny of this culture? What difference might it make to how we talk with this family if we permitted ourselves to hear Janet's oh-so-familiar account of "insight" within the context of the mother-blaming practices of this culture? And how might we proceed in our work if we allowed ourselves to recognize the extent to which psychotherapy has been complicit in the reproduction of this misogyny and a central player in the reproduction of mother-blame, if we allow ourselves to recognize the extent to which the culture of psychotherapy has reproduced the very context that is, in fact, constitutive of anorexia nervosa? And, in thinking about the education that family members have had in the course of their consultations about the solution to the problem, what might happen if we were to ask questions about what is here being reproduced by this so familiar story—by the cornerstone metaphors of the culture of psychotherapy; by the metaphors of individuation and differentiation and what stands in the shadows of these metaphors; versions of these metaphors that conflate individuation with separation and disengagement; versions of these metaphors that reproduce the isolated individualities that are so valorized in this culture?

I hope that this discussion goes some small way toward dispelling the assumption that the context of psychotherapy occu-

pies some privileged location apart from culture at large. This
assumption itself, and many other assumptions that are associated with it, play an entirely significant role in the construction
of a therapeutic stage that is not located at the periphery of
mainstream culture, but at its center. In occupying this location, therapy has played a cardinal role in the reproduction and
production of dominant culture. It has been a major player in
the maintenance of the dominant social order. It has made an
entirely significant contribution to the valorization of certain
ways of life and to the marginalization of other ways of life. In
regard to the hegemony of the lionized knowledges of this culture, psychotherapy has been duplicit.

I hope that this discussion also emphasizes the extent to which
we, as therapists, do not have to be condemned to the role of
unwitting accomplices in the reproduction of the dominant
social order. Although it is not possible for us to stand outside
of culture, we do not have to be wholly complicit with it. On
the other hand, however, the unquestioned acceptance of the
assumption that therapy occupies some privileged location apart
from culture at large guarantees that the practices of therapy will
be more complicit in the reproduction of the dominant culture.
The unquestioned acceptance of this assumption ensures the
duplication, in therapy, of the very context that is constitutive
of many of the problems that persons actually bring to therapy.

With these considerations, how might we experience therapeutic vanity? As folly. When we come to terms with the idea that
therapy is, in fact, in good part a performance of culture, the
question as to whether we, as therapists, bring politics into therapy becomes absurd. Accepting that psychotherapy cannot be
exempt from a role in the reproduction of this culture, coming
to terms with the fact that therapy is *of* this culture, permits us to
acknowledge the political dimensions and dilemmas of this work
as a given. We will acknowledge that when persons walk into our
consulting rooms, they will bring the relational politics of this

world with them. We will acknowledge that when persons walk into our consulting rooms, they walk into a political climate. We will acknowledge that as therapy is of this culture, as therapists, we will inevitably be playing a role in the reproduction of this culture. And we will be faced with new questions:

- What can we build into the therapeutic context that might contribute to our awareness of the politics of relationship?
- How do we propose to deal with the political dilemmas raised in this work?
- What steps can we take to avoid being wholly complicit in the reproduction of the dominant social order?
- What are some of the necessary conditions of a therapy that is sensitive to the politics of gender, heterosexual dominance, race, culture, class, and sexual orientation?
- How might we go about interacting with persons in ways that assist them to identify, to embrace, and to honor their resistance to those acts of self-government that they are incited to engage in by the dominant knowledges and practices of power in this modern culture?
- How might we go about subverting the hierarchies of knowledges that privilege professional knowledge claims and open up new possibilities for dissent?
- What possibilities are available to us for privileging alternative knowledges and the knowledgeableness of those persons who seek our help?
- How might we successfully confront ourselves with the moral and ethical responsibilities that we bear for the real effects of, or consequences of, our interactions with those persons who seek our help?
- What choices do we have in establishing structures that make our work accountable to those persons who seek our help—structures of accountability that might expose the real and the potential abuses in the practice of therapy?

- What are the appropriate ways for us to acknowledge the imbalance of power that is inherent in the therapeutic relationship?
- What actions can we take to mitigate the toxic effects of the imbalance of power that is inherent in the therapeutic relationship?
- How might we go about acknowledging our own location in the worlds of gender, race, class, culture, and sexual identity?
- And how might we go about acknowledging the implications of this location?

It is not possible, in the space of this chapter, for me to discuss all of these questions and their implications for therapy. So I restrict my discussion to just one of the practices of power in the culture of therapy. Below I review the real effects of the traditional and taken-for-granted one-way account of the therapeutic process.

CONSTITUTION OF THE THERAPIST'S LIFE

A one-way account of the therapeutic process is taken for granted in the culture of psychotherapy. The activities of the various organs of those institutions of the psychotherapy world are so clearly informed by the idea that the recipients of therapy are "solely" those persons who consult therapists, and that, if the therapy is successful, these persons will undergo some transformational processes. This is the case regardless of how therapists' contributions to such transformations might be conceived of—whether it be in terms of facilitating the conditions that might be favorable to such changes, whether it be in terms of the introduction of certain interventions, whether it be in terms of providing a new perspective on certain situations, or of engaging in certain processes of education, and so on. Therapeutic interaction is invariably represented as a one-way process. (An exception to this is when it is constructed in terms that are considered problematic, as for example, in the case of "countertransference.")

A critical review of the one-way account of this work exposes the workings and the reinforcement of the subject–object dualism that is so pervasive in the structuring of relations in Western culture. This dualism builds in the assumption that the therapist is an autonomous, detached, and knowing subject who has acquired certain "truth" knowledges, and that the person seeking help is the object of this knowledge. Therapists are conceived of as the actors or movers in this interaction that is called therapy, and those persons seeking help are defined as "other."

When engaging in this sort of critical review of therapeutic interaction, it becomes impossible to avoid the conclusion that the one-way representation of this process is marginalizing of those persons who seek help. It also becomes impossible to avoid the conclusion that there is a politics associated with the dominant conception of therapy as a one-way process, one that is associated with the construction and preservation of hierarchies of knowledge.

If we proceed to break from this subject–object dualism, we will be able to take seriously the notion that there can be no detached, autonomous position. We will be free to explore the implications of this understanding in our interactions with those persons who seek our help. This exploration will include acknowledgment of the extent to which therapeutic interaction is constitutive of the lives of all parties to this interaction; that what is shaping or constitutive of the lives of those persons who seek our help is also constitutive of what we commonly refer to as our work, and that what is shaping of our work is also constitutive of our lives in general.

This acknowledgment will be accompanied by the realization that it is an act of marginalization, an act that defines those persons who seek our help as "other," not to make it our business to identify, acknowledge, and articulate the ways in which this work changes our own lives. In this process of identifying, articulating, and acknowledging the extent to which this work is life-changing for therapists, I am not proposing some grand gesture, or, for that matter, something ingratiating. But I am suggesting an acknowledgment of the following:

- The privilege that we experience as persons invite us into their lives in various ways, and the real effects of this privilege on our own lives.
- The inspiration that we experience in this work as we witness persons changing their lives, despite formidable odds.
- The experience of new and special associations that enrich our lives.
- The joy that we experience as we are privy to the extent to which persons are able to intervene in their lives to bring about preferred changes, and as we join with persons in the celebration of these accomplishments.
- The special metaphors to which persons introduce us that provide us with thinking tools in other situations.
- How this interaction has enabled us to extend the limits of our thinking and to fill some of the gaps in our own self-narratives.
- The contribution that others make to the sustenance of our vision and our energy.

Such acknowledgment does play a significant role in dismantling the hierarchy of knowledges and the hierarchy of knowledgeableness. It usurps the taken-for-granted therapeutic arrangement. However, I do not believe that this is achieved at a cost to the therapist. How could this be a loss to us when it brings a new and different shape to therapeutic interaction, and new and different possibilities to our work with those persons who seek our help? In fact, as I have argued elsewhere, this acknowledgment actually *sustains* our work and powerfully authenticates our interest in people's lives and our curiosity about how things might be otherwise.

Perhaps I should clarify further how this acknowledgment sustains us. Have you ever experienced what is frequently referred to as burnout? Have you, at times, found your work exhausting or fatiguing? Have you ever experienced your work as directionless or lacking in purpose? Have there been periods in your life as a therapist that you would characterize as "treading water," or "just keeping your head above the surface"?

If your response to any of these questions is in the affirmative, then I would hazard a guess that at these times you have lost touch with a sense of the unfolding of preferred developments in your work. If a positive experience of direction in our work, of our therapy life going forward, of the viability of our purposes, is dependent upon this sense of the unfolding of preferred developments in our work—and I believe this to be the case—then surely not to recognize the ways in which this work changes our lives would play a very considerable role in denying us that which sustains our endeavor. How could we experience our therapy lives going forward in this way if we do not take the necessary steps to identify, acknowledge, and articulate our experience of the life-shaping nature of our interactions with others? Not to acknowledge this leads to a sense of being lost and bereft. So, I am suggesting that we have a choice. We can acknowledge that we are not lone actors, but working in collaboration with others, or we can all take Prozac.

ETHIC OF CONTROL

I have argued the implausibility of the notion that the therapeutic context is somehow sacrosanct; the notion that it occupies some privileged location, apart from culture at large. I have also argued that some awareness of the extent to which the culture of therapy reproduces the dominant culture can assist us in our search for a therapeutic posture that is not wholly complicit with the dominant culture; for a therapeutic posture that contributes to a revisioning of the therapeutic context, one that opens new possibilities for dissent. I believe that we can go some way toward extending this awareness and toward the revisioning of the therapeutic context by . . .

- Exploring the dominant ethic of our modern culture
- Understanding the link between this ethic and utopian visions of the social order
- Reviewing the development of modern practices of the government of people's lives.

Where might we begin this process? In embarking on the exploration of the dominant ethic of middle- and upper-middle-class life, which constitutes a significant majority of the professional class, it would be difficult to avoid confrontation with the modern ethic of control and contemporary notions of responsible action. I would here like to quote from Sharon Welch (1990) on the subject of this ethic:

> We assume that to be responsible means that one can ensure that the aims of one's action will be carried out. To act means to determine what will happen through that single action, to ensure that a given course of events will come to pass. This understanding of responsible action leads to a striking paralysis of will when faced with large, complex problems. It seems natural to many people, when faced with a problem too big to be solved alone or within the foreseeable future, simply to do nothing. (p. 3)

Here, I would like to explore the ways in which this ethic of control, and the account of responsible action that is associated with it, so often constitutes the lives of therapists, the lives of those persons who seek their help, and the therapeutic interaction itself.

In modern times, it has become increasingly difficult for us to avoid being attracted to the idea that we, as therapists, might, through independent and decisive action, bring about precipitous transformations in the lives of those persons who seek our help. Much of our training is oriented to this particular notion of responsible action, and much of what is published assumes this ethic of control. This notion severely compromises the capacity of therapists to persist in the face of problems and challenges that are of significant magnitude. If our definition of responsible action incites us to believe that we should be able to contribute independently, decisively, and immediately to the resolution of a problem, to the precipitation of some desired outcome, then it becomes entirely difficult for us to act at all when we find the size of a problem at all daunting, or when we are confronted with situations that are constructed as intractable, or when we find ourselves up against those powerful forces that support the status quo.

If we were to explore the links between, say, on the one hand, the practices of therapy that are informed by the ethic of control and the definition of responsible action that is associated with this ethic and, on the other hand, our experience of therapeutic interaction, I have no doubt that we would become aware of the link between our therapeutic practices and the "paralysis of will" that is reflected in the despair, demoralization, fatigue, resignation, cynicism, burnout, and jadedness that are so frequently reported by therapists. I quote further from Sharon Welch (1990), this time on the subject of despair:

> But this despair of the affluent, the despair of the middle class has a particular tone: it is a despair cushioned by privilege and grounded in privilege. It is easier to give up on long-term social

change when one is comfortable in the present—when it is possible to have challenging work, excellent health care and hous-
ing, and access to fine arts. When the good life is present or
within reach, it is tempting to despair of its ever being in reach
for others and resort merely to enjoying it for oneself and one's
family. . . . Becoming so easily discouraged is the privilege of
those accustomed to too much power, accustomed to having
needs met without negotiation and work, accustomed to having
a political and economic system that responds to their needs.
(p. 15)

Although at first it seems rather paradoxical, Welch proposes
that the extent to which we experience this "paralysis of will" is
determined by our relative positions in the social order; there
is a direct relationship between the extent to which we experience this paralysis of will and our location in the hierarchies
of privilege, knowledge, and power. Thus, we can assume that
men are more likely to experience this paralysis than women,
white races more than other races, members of the heterosexual community more than members of the homosexual and
lesbian communities, and so on. However, I suspect that very
few of us can be entirely exempt from the effects of this ethic
of control and this account of responsible action.

It goes without saying that a very great number of persons
who seek our help are not exempt from this ethic of control
either, and this makes it extremely difficult for them to take
steps toward the changes that they so want to achieve in their
lives. If success can be defined only by some immediate trans-
formation in one's circumstance, then this ethic invariably
incapacitates. It acts to obscure from people's view any of the
small steps that they might have made, or might have initiated
in establishing a context that is more favorable to, that is more
likely to prepare the way for, the changes that are considered
desirable. This ethic renders it virtually impossible for people

to honor and embrace the significance of such steps. It makes it entirely difficult for persons to relate to any of the more sparkling events of their own lives. Thus, change is so often forestalled, and resignation and despair are the outcomes.

If these persons, in their attempts to get help, first have to challenge and assist us to break from our own habits of thought and action that are associated with this ethic of control, including the "paralysis of will"—and I believe that this is so often required for the therapy to proceed—then, needless to say, they will be doubly burdened.

Implications for Therapy

A review of the ethic of control and the account of responsible action that accompanies it frees us to confront the resignation and despair that we might experience in our work with the persons who consult us. Such a review makes it possible for us to appreciate much of this resignation and despair as outcomes of a certain arrogance that is informed by the ethic of control. It affords us the opportunity to acknowledge and confront our privilege (in my case, as a white, middle-class, heterosexual man) as the context of this resignation and despair and, in so doing, faces us with new possibilities for breaking from the "paralysis of will." When we understand that the sort of influence that is proposed by the ethic of control is not possible, then we are encouraged to explore alternative notions of responsible action.

In challenging the ethic of control and its account of responsible action, it becomes more possible for us to assist persons to recognize, acknowledge, and honor the steps that they might be taking, or to explore the steps that might be available to them, in the generation of contexts that will be more favorable to the changes that they desire; those steps that provide the foundation of new possibilities in their lives. In working to break from the ethic of control, it becomes more possible for us to recognize and to name voices of dissent; to respect and name those actions that constitute a resistance to the dominant social order.

In questioning this ethic of control, we find that we are more able to acknowledge people's unique interpretations and negotiations of life, and more able to encourage them to do the same. We find that we are more able to bring forth the sense of personal agency involved in these unique interpretations and negotiations of life. And we find that we can become active in tracing alternative accounts of personal and relationship history that are associated with all of this; to juxtapose the dominant and imposed cultural plots with the counterplots of people's lives, with their histories of resistance.

When the persons who consult us have experienced forms of exploitation, abuse, and subjugation, the articulation and the elevation of the counter-plots of their lives brings with it a realization of the only partial success of the forces of domination; a realization of the extent to which the conquest of their lives was not total, and that it did not proceed unproblematically. Needless to say, this recognition has an entirely significant effect on the shape of people's lives and is critical to the development of possibilities for further acts of resistance.

This recognition provides for a different basis for action, one that Welch associates with the ethic of risk. This ethic is a basis of action that is not grounded in certainty but in the knowledge that outcomes cannot be assured, or, at times, even predicted; a basis for responsible action in conjunction with the acknowledgment that control is impossible; a basis for responsible action that is grounded in an appreciation of the resources that persons can depend upon to see themselves through; a basis for responsible action that is informed by the understanding that persons cannot act morally alone, outside of contexts of accountability and collaboration.

Responsibility

The version of responsibility associated with this work is one that emphasizes accountability. It involves a commitment to establish therapy as a context in which we are accountable to those persons who seek our help; accountable for how we think, for what we do, and for the real effects or consequences of our interactions with those persons who seek our help.

This is not a context in which therapists can presume a position of neutrality, a context in which therapists can hold out a claim to a space that is free of the relations of power and of the biases associated with their location in the social world. This is not a context in which it is possible for therapists to entertain an "objective" position in this work; to transcend their ways of being and thinking that are informed by culture, class, race, and gender. Instead, it is a context of accountability that encourages . . .

- Therapists to render visible certain aspects of their taken-for-granted ways of being and thinking, to expand their consciousness of their biases.
- Therapists to acknowledge their location in the social world, and the privileges and the limits of understanding that are associated with this location.
- Therapists to acknowledge the assumptions and purposes that are associated with those metaphors that guide their work.
- Persons to confront the limits of their therapists' understandings and to express their experience of these limits.
- Persons to honor the unique understandings and experiences of life that pertain to their location in the world of gender, race, class, culture.
- Therapists to transgress the limits of their thought by stepping into alternative sites of culture.

This notion of responsibility emphasizes responsibility for the real effects of our actions and interactions within the context of therapy itself.

Pathologizing

I am also referring to the sort of responsibility that includes a refusal to engage in the politics of totalization and marginalization of persons' lives, a refusal to enter into the ever-expanding discourses of psychopathology that so saturate the culture of therapy. (Have you caught up with the recent developments?: ODD, Oppositional Defiant Disorder, and DD, Defiant Disorder, which I am led to believe is worse.)

To engage in these expert internalizing discourses of psychopathology is political in several senses. First, in that these discourses internalize the locus of the problems that persons bring to therapy, they erase the historical forces that are constitutive of these problems, and they deny a political analysis of the context that is constitutive of the problem. In short, these discourses of psychopathology render invisible the politics of experience. This has the effect of incapacitating those persons who seek our help. The pathologizing of life subtracts from personal agency. It has the effect of privileging the expert knowledges and disqualifying the knowledgeableness of those persons who seek our help. It subtracts from a sense of personal agency, and it makes it virtually impossible for persons to identify, to embrace, to honor, and to extend their acts of resistance to those historical forces and political processes that are constitutive of the problems for which they seek therapy.

Second, in trafficking in the expert discourses on psychopathology, and in perfecting the reproduction of these discourses in their interactions with others, therapists are engaging in a particular presentation of their "self" that will accord them a significant grant of moral worth within particular institutions and communities of persons. In these institutions and communities, other ways of speaking about lives are discriminated against and marginalized. These modern ways of speaking about life constitute modern rituals of exclusion.

Third, the expert discourses on psychopathology contribute to a "psychologization" of life that acts as a panacea for the concerns of therapists. As this psychologization serves to obscure, for therapists, the extent to which the problems that persons bring to therapy are mired in relational politics—in practices of power and in structures of domination—it brings with it a certain degree of comfort for therapists. In making it possible for us to define certain problems as an aberration rather than a product of our modes of life and thought, we are able to avoid facing our complicity in the maintenance of those aspects of these ways of life and thought that are constitutive of the very problems that persons bring to therapy.

Take, for example, the therapy of those men who perpetrate abuse. To pathologize these men, to see them as aberrant, would enable me, as a man, to obscure the link between the violence of these men and the dominant ways of being and thinking for men in this culture that valorize aggression, domination, and conquest. It would enable me, as a man, to avoid confronting the ways in which I might be complicit in the reproduction of these dominant ways of being and thinking. It would enable me, as a member of the class of men, to avoid facing the responsibility that I have to take action to contribute to the dismantling of men's privilege that perpetuates inequality of opportunity, to the destabilization of the structures of oppression, and to the challenging of the various practices of power that subjugate and marginalize others. And it would enable me to continue to leave it to those persons in the least powerful position to raise issues of disqualification, discrimination, and so on, and to take action to end this.

Fourth, the psychologization of life that is achieved by the professional knowledges supports the assumption of therapist objectivity and preserves the myth of therapist impartiality, detachment, and neutrality. This psychologization of life is achieved through a network of universal truth claims that obscures the extent to which professional knowledges are culture-specific and the extent to which they are manufactured through specific historical and political processes. In reviewing the real effects of the psychologizing practices on therapists' interactions with those persons who consult them, we can discern the extent to which these practices . . .

- Render invisible our location in the worlds of gender, race, class, ethnicity, and so on.
- Make it possible for us to avoid facing the moral and ethical responsibility for the real effects or consequences of our interactions with those persons who seek our help.
- Assist us to disavow our complicity in the production of the worlds that we share with others.
- Encourage us to embrace the notion that our thoughts and actions can be free of "contamination" derived from our cultural and social location in the world, and in doing so support the very subject–object dualism that preserves the hierarchies of knowledge, knowledgeableness, and power.

RELATIVISM

Some critiques of recent developments in social theory—those that encourage us to break from the ethic of control, that challenge us to eschew foundational ideas about the nature of the world, including utopian notions of an ideal life in an ideal state—argue that this leaves us no choice but to embrace relativism. Usually these critiques argue that relativism gives no basis for action. There is no foundational truth idea to which we might refer to take action; there is no recourse to the nature of the world, to some universal law; there is no religious support, and there are no guarantees about outcome.

Some postfoundationalist thinkers, who conceive of relativism as a radical idea, would agree with this state and, in fact, enjoin us to celebrate it. They would argue that the only basis for action is subjective. Here, I will argue that relativism is distinctly conservative, and that the very notion of relativism as a basis for life is, in itself, the outcome of the ethic of control.

Relativism is conservative because it ignores the inequality of access to resources, the structures of power that privilege some voices over other voices, the rules about which forms of speech are valorized, about who is to speak about what and in what circumstances. Relativism serves to legitimate the domination of others, and it preserves the status quo. Relativism assumes that the individual actor can be a moral agent, and it is also somewhat blind to the constitutive nature of any action. Foundationalism is conservative because it is normative. Instead of embracing relativism, from this perspective we would argue for a review of the real effects of this idea, in order that we might more clearly see the purposes to which it is being put.

I would argue that the idea of basing action on foundational truths *and* the idea of basing action on relativist notions are *both* part of the ethic of control. Both propose a basis for action that is an individual matter. This is precisely the sort of action that I am not proposing. I am proposing action based on a different ethic, an ethic of accountability. This is an argument for action as a process, action that emerges from material interactions with persons who are at different sites of this culture. This is action that is based on neither foundationalism nor relativism. This ethic would guide our work in a number of ways:

1. We would make it our business to build in structures that assist us to hold ourselves morally accountable for the real effects of our interactions on the lives of others.

2. We would establish contexts that would assist us to critique the normative ideas that we hold.
3. We would identify the structures of power and domination and act to dismantle them.
4. We would recognize that adequate moral critique can be arrived at only through our material interactions with persons and different communities of persons, through the interaction of different principles, norms, and mores.

Yes, undoubtedly the foundations for action are through dialogue, but just not through any dialogue.

CONCLUSION

Like all of you, at times I get asked the question, "Why do you do therapy?" During my social work training, which was in the heyday of structuralist thought, students were encouraged to psychologize their motives for joining what was referred to then as a "helping profession." This psychologization of motive invariably translated into a pathologizing of motive. Did one's motive for taking up social work relate to unresolved issues in one's family of origin? Was it to do with an "enmeshed" relationship with one's mother and the intensity of her injunction to be helpful? Was it to do with a lack of closeness in one's relationship with one's mother and an attempt to rectify one's sense of failure to be appropriately helpful? Was it to do with the rejection of the expectations of one's father? Was it to do with an absence of expectations from one's father? And, what was the hidden, unconscious, and unacknowledged self-interest that was being served by this decision? Which of all of one's neurotic needs were being met by this decision? (Or the questioning centered around what had been reinforced—the stimulus–response paradigm.) I once did a survey and discovered that the very same questions that pathologize motive were also frequently asked of persons entering the other so-called helping professions, so I am sure that many of you could draw from your experience and add to this list of questions.

The fact that I was interested in counseling, and family therapy in particular, was seen as a confirmation of some of the suspicions inherent in these sorts of questions. However, it always occurred to me that such questions informed deeply conservative interpretations of motive, and that these interpretations of motive had real consequences for the careers of many of the persons who had chosen to work in this field.

Back then, conscious purpose had relatively bad press (and, I might add, still does), so much so that statements of conscious purpose were considered irrelevant. And to connect one's motive for choosing this career to some form of commitment aroused intense suspicion. It was considered that notions of commitment had their roots in defensiveness and that the maintenance of such notions could only be attributed to a lack of insight.

Now, this psychologization of motive seemed particularly bizarre during a time when Australia was involved in the Vietnam war, and considering that a number of us were engaged in protesting Australian and American participation in this war. Although there were certainly rifts, many students and others were galvanized in this protest, and much of the effective action that was taken depended on this. The statements of conscious purpose and notions of commitment seemed critical to this achievement, and they were honored, not pathologized. Can you imagine what would have happened to the whole movement had we all sat down and psychologized our motives for engaging in these protests!

Most of you are aware of the extent of the demoralization that has been experienced in the helping professions in recent times. Of course, this demoralization has many roots, and I have referred to just some of these in the above discussion. I can't help but think that another entirely significant factor in this demoralization is the psychologizing and pathologizing of motive that has dominated the past two or three decades. I believe that these interpretations have had their real effects in the constitution of the lives of therapists, effects that are deeply conservative and have contributed to the "paralysis of will" referred to earlier.

So, perhaps it is now time for us to find new ways of recuperating statements of conscious purpose, and to elevate these statements so that they are more constitutive of our lives and our work. And perhaps it is now time for us to reclaim notions of commitment and, together, find ways of helping each other to honor such notions (commitments to address injustice, not commitments to some utopian ideal).

So I do hope that I have gone some way toward having my say about what this is about for me. But this is not all, and I would like to share just one more thought about this, one that also relates to another account of motive, one that is also non-pathologizing. Michel Foucault once said in an interview: "The main interest in life and work is to become someone else that you were not in the beginning. If you knew when you began a book what you would say at the end, do you think that you would have the courage to write it? What is true for writing and for a love relationship is true also for life" (1982, quoted in Martin et al., 1988, p. 9).

I appreciate this sentiment and would translate it this way: If you knew, when you entered a therapeutic interaction, where you would be at the end—if you knew beforehand the particularities of how this was going to be life-changing for you—do you think that you would have the courage to keep doing it?

CHAPTER 4

"Countertransference" and Rich Story Development

From time to time, therapists are touched by their work in ways that unsettle. At these times they can find themselves feeling bewildered, hurt, disappointed, and despairing. Therapists may find themselves experiencing powerful emotions toward the people seeking consultation, and they may attribute negative motives to these people. On some of these occasions therapists are being subjected to acts of power that are disqualifying or diminishing of them. On other occasions, these painful experiences are the outcome of what is often referred to as "countertransference." This is considered a phenomenon in which repressed and often forgotten emotions are being directed by the therapist at people who seek consultation. In the first case, it is important to assist the therapist in identifying and naming the operations of power to which he or she is being subjected, and to encourage him or her to find appropriate ways of explicitly addressing this exposé in the context of the therapeutic conversations. In the second case, the "countertransference" phenomenon can provide a point of entry to rich story development for the therapist.

RICH STORY DEVELOPMENT

When therapists seek consultation over "countertransference" phenomena, one option available to the consultant is to consider this response a point of entry for rich story development. In this case, the consultant might first encourage the therapist to identify (1) the expressions to which he or she is responding and (2) what these are expressions of. Special attention is given to an inquiry into what these expressions suggest about what is given value to or what is held precious. For example:

- A direct expression of something that is highly valued by the therapist,
- The expression of a lament over the absence of something highly valued, or
- An expression of pain or suffering that is implicitly suggestive of something that is valued but absent.

The consultant supports the therapist in the rich characterization of what has been identified in terms of what is accorded value. The consultant then interviews the therapist about . . .

- The images of life and identity that are evoked in this rich characterization of what is accorded value.
- The resonances in the history of the therapist's lived experience that are set off by these images.
- What these resonances reflect about what the therapist has accorded value to in the history of his or her life.
- How the therapist has maintained a relationship with what he or she has accorded value.

This exploration sets the scene for the wider acknowledgment of what the therapist has preserved as precious and of how he or she has preserved this. This also sets the scene for the therapist to acknowledge, to the people seeking consultation, the ways in which his or her life has been touched by their expressions.

An Example

For example, in my supervision meeting with Judy, she was talking about what was really unsettling to her in her work with a newly referred family. In these conversations, she'd experienced what she said was a "negative psychological reaction" that she found quite painful. She couldn't figure this out. In these conversations, she hadn't been really aware of anything that could account for her negative reaction to the family with which she was working. In her efforts to resolve this situation, she was aware that she'd begun to manufacture some negative interpretations of the family members' motives, but in doing this, she felt that she was compromising her own values.

So I invited Judy into a conversation that would make some meaning out of this experience. I encouraged her to try and distinguish which of the family's *expressions* she might be responding to, that might in some way relate to what she termed a "negative psychological reaction." I also asked her to describe the sort of *images of life and identity* that might be triggered by these expressions. The third step was to get her to speculate about what it was in the history of her own lived experience that might be *resonating* with this expression of the family. I then wanted her to reflect on the ways in which this was, in some ways, *transporting* to her, or moving her.

Now, in endeavoring to find to what she was responding, Judy became aware that she'd been drawn to some very significant expressions of acceptance of the daughter by the parents in this family. Something like a reunion had taken place in the context of the therapeutic conversation itself: The daughter had been split off from the family, and she'd agreed to come to this meeting, and so a reunion had taken place in Judy's presence. In describing the images that had been evoked by this event, and in tracing the history of these, Judy became aware of how they had awakened a very contrasting experience for her: painful memories of rejection that she'd felt from her own parents. I asked her about why this rejection was so painful to her, and about why this pain had arisen in the context of her work with this particular family. Judy gave voice to a powerful longing for recognition and acceptance, and identified the longing as the foundation of her painful experience. She'd had this powerful longing for recognition and acceptance, but this was something that she was not generally conscious of and that she rarely publicly acknowledged. So that's what this family's interaction had touched on so powerfully for her.

There is always an "absent but implicit" in expressions—experiences of psychological pain are *in relation to* something. In a way, the response is a testimony to what people hold precious; pain is always *in relation to* something. So, in some ways, Judy's pain was a testimony to what it was she held precious: a longing for recognition and acceptance. It was clear to me that Judy had held onto this longing for recognition and acceptance despite the difficult experiences she'd had in her family. I wanted to know how she'd sustained this longing for recognition and acceptance right through her life. After some discussions, Judy began to recall a connection with the parents of one of her school friends. For a time, these parents had included Judy in aspects of their family life in ways that made her feel recognized and accepted. This inclusion came to a sudden end when Judy's family relocated to another part of town, and so she lost contact with these parents of her school friend.

Now, Judy assumed that it would be possible to discover the whereabouts of these parents of her school friend, and she was enthusiastic about the prospects of informing them of the significance of their act of inclusion of her when she was just a young girl. Something about this act of inclusion had helped her to maintain a relationship with this longing for acceptance. She hadn't abandoned this; she'd held onto it. She believed that this action of informing them of their contribution would constitute a further expression of this longing, and an acknowledgment of it, and that this would be helpful to her. She thought this would be quite transporting of her—to meet with the parents of this old school friend and acknowledge their contribution to her life, to acknowledge their part in her maintenance of this longing. She also formulated a plan for acknowledging, to the members of the family who were consulting with her, the ways her life had been touched by their expressions. Through a relatively brief search, Judy got in touch with the parents of her old school friend, and she had a wonderful reunion with them. And, at the end of her work with the family, Judy was able to acknowledge their contribution to her life—that this contact had opened up some possibilities for the acknowledgment of this longing, and opened up a possibility for her to take action that contributed to her having a renewed sense of personal intimacy and warmth.

To me, this is a story about how we might pick up on what's often referred to as "countertransference." I'm really interested in this phenomenon. I'm interested in the expressions to which the therapist is responding, and I'm interested in what the therapist experiences as unsettling or painful might be speaking to, in terms of what the therapist values highly. As I said, there is always an "absent but implicit": We are "unsettled" in relation to something that would settle us. I'm always interested in what that might be. And so, with Judy, I interviewed her about the *images of life and identity* that were evoked by this. I wanted to know about the *resonances in her personal history* that were triggered by these images. I also wanted to know what these reflected regarding to *what she gave value*, and then I wanted to know how she'd *maintained a relationship* with that to which she gave value. And this set the scene for a wider acknowledgment of what Judy had preserved over this time as a therapist. It also set the scene for her to acknowledge to this newly referred family the ways in which they'd touched her life. What I'm trying to suggest here is that what's often referred to as "countertransference" can open the door to what I often refer to as rich story development and rich acknowledgments.

CHAPTER 5

The Resistances and Therapist Responsibility

Resistance is an interpretation that is applied by therapists to a range of phenomena. On account of this, it is more appropriate to speak of resistance in the plural—to refer to "resistances." For example, the interpretation of resistance might be valid when a therapist has attempted to proceed in ways that are inappropriate on account of . . .

- A lack of sensitivity to the cultural and ethnic contexts of people's lives.
- A limited consciousness of the politics of local culture; for example, the politics of race, class, heterosexism, gender (including gender reassignment), disadvantage, and marginalization because of disability and disenfranchisement.
- The unwitting sponsorship of the norms of the contemporary world in ways that disqualify diversity in people's everyday lives.
- The imposition of theoretical understandings of life, to which people do not relate.
- The introduction of solutions that are discordant with what people value in life and with what they intend for their lives.

In these circumstances, "resistance" is a sign that the therapist should pause to engage in consultations with the people who are seeking his or her help, and with other consultants, in order to:

- Acknowledge the significance of this resistance.
- Raise their consciousness of these considerations.
- Foreground these considerations in conversations about the predicaments that people bring to therapy, and about people's experience of therapy.
- Seek more collaborative ways of proceeding.

Resistance is also frequently an interpretation made in response to what is perceived as a rejection of the therapist's efforts to assist people in making changes that are clearly desired by them. There are many explanations for this phenomenon, including those that assert that this is because people are invested in the preservation of the status quo.

NATURE OF CHANGE

The changes that are required of people in successfully addressing their predicaments are usually quite significant. And changing significant aspects of one's life is a sophisticated achievement. This is an achievement that requires people to (1) traverse the space between what is known and familiar about their lives to what it is possible for them to know and to do (a space that often presents as a chasm), and to (2) derive an enhanced sense of personal agency.

Personal agency is the outcome of the development of a sense of self that is associated with the perception that one is able to have some effect on the shape of one's own life; that is, a sense that (1) one is able to intervene in one's own life as an agent of what one gives value to and as an agent of one's own intentions, and (2) the world is at least minimally responsive to the fact of one's existence. Following the Russian psychologist, Lev Vygotsky, this gap between the known and familiar and what it is possible to know and do can be understood as the "zone of proximal development." In his research, Vygotsky (1986) principally focused on early childhood learning. But this consideration of the "zone of proximal development" is relevant for learning at all stages and ages.

ZONE OF PROXIMAL DEVELOPMENT

For Vygotsky, all learning is a social and relational achievement; it is the outcome of a social collaboration that contributes to the scaffolding of this zone of proximal development. In this scaffolding, people are supported in manageable learning tasks as they incrementally and progressively gain distance from the known and familiar toward what is possible for them to know and do. These learning tasks can be categorized as:

1. Low-level distancing tasks; that is, tasks that encourage people to characterize specific objects and events of their worlds.
2. Medium-level distancing tasks; that is, tasks that encourage people to bring into relationship specific objects and events of their world in the development of chains of association, or "complexes," that establish bonds and relations between these objects and events.
3. Medium-high-level distancing tasks; that is, tasks that encourage people to reflect on these chains of association and to draw from these realizations and learnings about specific phenomena.
4. High-level distancing tasks; that is, tasks that encourage people to abstract these realizations and learnings from

their concrete and specific circumstances in the formation of concepts about life and identity.

5. Very-high-level distancing tasks; that is, tasks that encourage the formulation of predictions about the outcome
of specific actions founded upon this concept development, and tasks that encourage the planning for and ini-
tiation of such actions.

This concept development, which is the outcome of collaborative learning, provides the principal foundation for
people to regulate their own lives and relationships. It is this
concept development that provides the basis for a sense of
personal agency.

THERAPEUTIC PRACTICE

The therapeutic task is to contribute to the scaffolding of the
proximal zone of development. This scaffolding makes it possible for people to incrementally and progressively distance
themselves from the known and familiar toward what it might
be possible for them to know and to do.

Actions that might be interpreted as a rejection of the
therapist's efforts to assist people to make changes that are
clearly desired by them are understood to be expressions
of the extent to which these people (1) are mired in the
known and familiar, and (2) are not experiencing the sort of
social collaboration that would effectively scaffold the zone
of proximal development. In this circumstance, the therapist is alerted to the fact that he or she has not been fully
present with his or her scaffolding skills, or that he or she
has reached the limits of these skills in consultations with
particular people in relation to specific issues.

Some phenomena that are often understood to be "resistance" either serve as a wake-up call to the therapist, or light

up the limits of the therapist's skill, encouraging him or her to explore ways of extending on these limits. I'd like to give just a brief example of this.[1] I was working with one young man who was in lots of trouble; he was considered to "lack insight," and to be a "concrete thinker." He was understood to have an inability to predict the consequences of his actions. He was in trouble with the police, with the school, with his family—and the family was now considering fostering him out. When I sat down with him and his family and asked him a few questions, it became clear to me that I needed to play a very significant role in scaffolding the space between what was known and familiar to him, and what was possible for him to know and do, because he didn't have any *concepts* about life or identity that would provide a foundation for him to experience personal agency, for him to intervene in the shaping of his own life.

Now, in this conversation, for the first time he gave value to a word that was known to him. I'll give a brief account of how this happened. This young man was split off from his family, and I wanted to know what were the consequences of that for him. He'd never given voice to those consequences; he'd never taken them into a relationship with his actions. So, I invited him to reflect on this: What was his experience of this development of being split off from the family and its consequences? He said he wasn't too happy about this. This was the first time he'd actually had a foundation upon which to reflect. The next step was to ask him *why* he wasn't so happy about this, and he just shrugged his shoulders. So I asked his mother, "Well, what's your guess about why Freddy's so unhappy about this?" She said, "Because of what he'll miss out on." I asked, "What's that?" and she said, "Belonging." I then turned and asked Freddy, "Does that fit with you?" and he nodded his head and used the word "belonging" for the first time. So I asked, "Well, Freddy, what do you mean by *belonging?*" and he gradually took over this concept. At the end of the interview, he talked about how all of the violence that he was actually perpetrating in other peoples' lives was "borrowing" his belonging, and he wasn't happy about it borrowing his belonging. So *belonging* had now become a concept for him. He now had a foundation for taking action in relation to all of these predicaments that had been caused by his actions and his violence.

I think it's our task to contribute to the scaffolding of the zone of proximal development. This scaffolding enables people to have the opportunity to take up words that are familiar to them and develop these into concepts about life and about identity. According to Vygotsky, it's *concept development* that makes it possible for us to proceed with life. It makes it possible for us to regulate our life in some way.

One of the points that I'd like to make here is that so often we interpret it as "resistance" when the people who are consulting us experience a *failure to know,* or experience a failure to know *what to do.* And I think that's our responsibility. I think if people are experiencing that sense of being a failure to know, then we're responsible for that in some way; we haven't provided enough scaffolding for them to actually know what they might be able to know about their own lives. So I think this encourages us to reflect on what we're doing: Maybe we've been a bit neglectful in terms of being fully present with our skills. Or maybe we're up against the limits of what we know in terms of providing that sort of scaffold, and we need to find ways of extending on those limits through consultations with colleagues and others. I think that, so often, the interpretation of "resistance" is made when the person consulting the therapist has no clue about how to get to where he or she wants to get to from where they are. It's such a chasm. I think it's very important that we provide the sort of collaboration that can make it possible for people to incrementally and progressively distance themselves from what is known and familiar to them, to reveal what might be possible for them to know. In this way, I think the concept of "resistance" actually encourages us to reflect on our skills in this work.

EDITOR'S NOTE

1. A thorough account of this example of therapeutic practice is provided in Chapter 8.

PART II

Special Topics
in Therapy

CHAPTER 6

On Anorexia

AN INTERVIEW WITH MICHAEL WHITE

Narrative therapists who work with people who are trying to reclaim their lives from anorexia nervosa often use externalizing practices in this work. Can you explain why these practices are significant in this context?

Externalizing conversations assist people to characterise whatever problem they are dealing with. This characterization takes place in ways that are near to the person's own experience. People are supported in finding their own words and their own metaphors to achieve this characterization. One of the purposes of assisting people to achieve this is to render tangible that which is usually relatively intangible. Without such characterization, problems like anorexia can be experienced as all-pervasive. When problems like anorexia remain intangible, it is virtually impossible for people to distinguish the sphere of influence of the problem, to distinguish where it starts and where it finishes. Through externalizing conversations, problems become bounded. These conversations contribute to the sort of characterization of a problem that establishes its boundaries or borders. The problem becomes a distinct entity, and the outcome of this is that it ceases to represent the totality of a person's life.

Is the aim to name the problem in one distinct way?

I believe that it is important for therapists to spend time "loitering" in the early part of these externalizing conversations so that the problem is not just named but also richly characterized. It is my understanding that this is one of the primary aims of these conversations—to develop a rich, externalized characterization of the problem. In this characterization, it is usually the case that the problem is named in a multiplicity of ways. In my experience, it is rare that the problem is named in singular terms.

Because "anorexia nervosa" is the popular definition of what it is that many women and some men are struggling with, this definition is often selected for rich characterization at the outset of externalizing conversations. But people do not have identical experiences of whatever anorexia nervosa is, and invariably people also employ a range of other descriptions in these externalizing conversations. These can include descriptions such as "perfectionism" or "fastidiousness" or "expectations." As the conversations develop over the course of therapeutic sessions, these externalized definitions often "drift" through a range of descriptions. This drift is the outcome of ongoing attention to supporting the generation of experience-near definitions that are most relevant to people's current encounters with the problem.

What comes next?

The sort of inquiry that contributes to this characterization of problems encourages people to orient themselves to their problems as "investigative reporters." This role can then be extended by supporting people to develop a detailed account of the consequences of anorexia nervosa (or of whatever definition is preferred), of the operations and activities of this problem, of the consequences of these operations and activities to the person's life, and an account of what these consequences might reflect about the "agenda" of the problem for the person's life and relationships.

In the yet further development of this investigative reporter role, people can be encouraged to develop an exposé of the contexts of life that sponsor anorexia nervosa. This would be an exposé of the discourses of life and identity that foster anorexia nervosa, including the practices of the self and practices of relationship that are associated with these discourses, and of the complicity of social institutions in this. Externalizing conversations of this sort are well-suited to bring forth the politics of people's experience of these forces, and I regard this also to be a priority in therapeutic practice.

What sorts of metaphors emerge in these externalizing conversations to describe the person's relationship with anorexia nervosa?

Avoiding the imposition of metaphors to describe the person's relationship with anorexia nervosa is a key consideration. The development of externalizing conversations is not founded on a proposal for introducing a ready-made characterization of the problem, or a ready-made characterization of the person's relationship with the problem. Just as people will employ a range of definitions of the problems that they bring to therapy, they will also employ a range of metaphors to characterize their relationships with these problems. In the context of externalizing conversations, people are encouraged to develop these metaphors in the definition of their relationships with their problems, and to monitor the consequences of the utilisation of these metaphors in their efforts to address these problems.

I don't believe that it is our place, as therapists, to take a lead role in defining people's relationships with their problems.

While I do not believe that it is our place to impose metaphors to define people's relationships with their problems, I do think that we have a significant responsibility in terms of the metaphors that we choose to join with. For example, a person might employ battle or contest metaphors to describe his or her relationship with anorexia—"I am fighting for my survival," "This is a struggle to the death," "I have to vanquish anorexia"—but these will not be the only metaphors taken up in the definition of this relationship, and these will not be the only metaphors that define the task. It is common for people to also employ other metaphors, and it is important that we listen for these. For example, alongside the battle/contest metaphors, people will speak about how they want to get their lives back from anorexia nervosa, which is a "reclaiming" metaphor. Or a person might make mention of the questions that he or she has about the restrictions of the anorexia lifestyle, and these questions are often couched in metaphors of protest. Or a person might talk about salvaging his or her life, which is a marine metaphor. Or the therapist might hear something in the conversation that hints at a geological metaphor—for example, the person might give expression to his or her quest by proposing steps to undermine the influence of anorexia nervosa. It is my experience that people usually employ several metaphors in characterizing their relationship with their problems and in characterizing the task at hand.

Are all these different metaphors associated with different effects, different possibilities, different hazards?

Yes. The metaphors that people take up in characterizing their relationship with problems will significantly shape their actions and their experience. And these metaphors will also have a significant influence on the intensity of people's relationship with their problems. For example, in the context of addressing anorexia nervosa, battle and contest metaphors will sponsor an intense relationship with the problem. These metaphors will sponsor a hot engagement with anorexia nervosa. Other metaphors will sponsor an engagement that is much less intense, and that will be more conducive to the further development of the investigative reporter posture that I have already mentioned.

This investigative reporter posture sponsors a more detached relationship with the problem. Although investigative reporters usually do have a political agenda, they are not locked into battle with an adversary. In the context of therapeutic conversations regarding anorexia nervosa, this investigative reporter posture makes it possible for people to develop an extensive exposé of the problem, of the discourses associated with it, of the operations and activities linked to and informed by these discourses, and of the problem's sociopolitical context. When I speak of a detached relationship, I am not referring to an "academic" position in which one is detached from one's experience. To the contrary, these externalizing conversations open possibilities for people to render visible the politics of their experience, and to give fuller expression to this. The investigative reporter posture also provides people with a platform from which it is more possible for them to make decisions about what steps they might take to reclaim their lives, or to undermine the influence of anorexia nervosa, or to protest its requirements of them, or however the task might be defined by these alternative metaphors.

The concerns associated with anorexia nervosa—about body image, about one's thoughts, one's desires, one's emotional expressions, one's posture, one's gestures, and so on—usually sponsor a pretty intense relationship between the person and the problem. Metaphors that redouble the intensity of people's engagement with anorexia nervosa run the risk of contributing to the possibility that anorexia nervosa will become an even greater distracting force.

But what if the person describes themselves as in a battle for their life or in warfare against anorexia nervosa?

At times, metaphors that evoke battle, or conquest, or a fight for survival, are employed by people who are experiencing anorexia nervosa. Such a metaphor may represent anorexia nervosa as a tyrant that is attempting to oppress the person's life. And it is important that any experience of "fighting for one's survival" be honored. In raising concerns about these battle/contest metaphors, I am not suggesting that they be disqualified when they are employed by people to define their relationship with their problems. I believe it is possible to acknowledge these experiences, and to appreciate the significance of defining one's relationship with the problem in this way. But there are hazards associated with a singular sponsorship of such metaphors, and with the neglect of some of the other metaphors that are also employed by people to define this relationship with the problem and the task at hand.

The effect of increasing the intensity of the person's relationship with anorexia nervosa is one of these hazards. But there are other hazards. For instance, if the quest is to vanquish the problem, then what happens if it rises up again, even in a mild way? Will this resurgence be understood in terms of having lost the battle or having failed in the contest? If so, this could inadvertently reinforce a sense of hopelessness or futility, or a sense of personal failure or inadequacy or incompetence. As well, many of these battle/contest metaphors run the risk of contributing to further isolation in circumstances in which the lifestyle associated with anorexia nervosa is already a quite isolated one. The further development of these metaphors can lead to a fortress-type mentality that can exacerbate a sense of personal vulnerability and personal isolation. As well as this, I believe that we have ethical concerns about contributing to the further development of these battle/contest metaphors in the context of therapeutic conversations. Do we wish to contribute to the development of discourses of life that are shaped by battle and contest metaphors?

If a person does characterize his or her relationship with anorexia nervosa in terms of a battle or contest, it is possible to be respectful of this representation and to fully honor it, without making a significant contribution to the further development of such metaphors. Even when battle or conquest metaphors are significantly present in a conversation, there will be other metaphors present as well, and many of these are not as potentially hazardous.

Why is it significant not to contribute to a "fortress-type mentality"?

If we are not careful, we may inadvertently respond to those who are struggling with any problem in ways that increase their sense of isolation and vulnerability rather than decrease it, in ways that escalate a sense of susceptibility rather than diminish it. For example, a therapist could inadvertently contribute to this if the discourses of victimhood are significantly shaping his or her contribution to the therapeutic conversations. A person might report being split off from friends on account of trauma that he or she has experienced, and on account of a perception that these friends don't understand, or on account of experiencing expectations from the friends to be quickly over this trauma. A sense of isolation and personal vulnerability will be fostered when therapists respond to this predicament by underscoring what they determine to be the inadequacies of these friends, or by constructing their actions as a form of betrayal or disqualification. And the exacerbation of this sense of vulnerability can lead to the development of what I have referred to as a "fortress-type mentality," in which the person derives a sense that he or she is evermore at risk of being impinged upon by negative forces from the external world. In this development the therapist becomes centered in the person's life in a way that has the effect of diminishing this person's sense of personal agency.

This potential for therapeutic conversations to inadvertently contribute to personal isolation and a sense of vulnerability, and to unintentionally promote a "fortress-type mentality," is something for all therapists to maintain a healthy conscious-ness of. This is particularly important when therapists are con-sulted by people who are dealing with anorexia nervosa.

Whenever a fortress-type mentality is developed in therapeu-tic conversations, there is a tendency for the person consulting the therapist to be constructed as either "victim" or as "hero." Both concepts can be debilitating. "Self as hero" can be an equally isolating concept. If people are represented as heroes, standing up to an overpowering adversary, this construction can contribute to furthering an ideal image of a "perfect self"—one that is self-possessed, self-contained, self-resourcing, and so on. These sorts of understandings of identity can be very limiting and isolating, and they are linked to the very understandings of life that may have contributed to the development of anorexia nervosa in the first place.

What if there are aspects of anorexia or the anorectic lifestyle that the person appreciates?

Actually, it is rare for people to take a total position on a problem. When involved in externalizing conversations, they characterize the problem, they provide an account of the con-sequences of the problem in their lives, and we then use these statements as a reflection to support further characterization of the problem. Questions might be asked, such as, "What does this say about the problem's intentions for your life—its purposes or its plans for the future?" And then we interview the person about the experience of the problem and its consequences. Very often, the person does not take a total position. Most times, there are some aspects of the consequences of the problem to which the person is drawn, and there are many aspects to which the person is not. It is not a total position.

To recognize this point is really important. It means that what we are doing is privileging the voices of these people in providing an account of their experience in all its complexity. They are able to speak about the aspects of anorexia or their current lifestyle that are problematic, such as the isolation or the extent to which the consequences of the problem are restricting them from making an appearance in life physically, intellectually, mentally, emotionally, socially. But often the person is also able to speak about some aspects of life associated with anorexia nervosa that are linked with certain aesthetics of living to which they are very drawn. These are aesthetics of living that are linked to what they intend for their life and to what they give value. If we do not want to alienate people from the therapeutic context, then honoring these distinctions is very important.

What does honoring these distinctions make possible?

If people have to be all for anorexia or all against it, it makes it really hard for them. If they have to take a position that is total, then doing so may contribute to a great deal of anxiety and a great deal of apprehension about any step they might take to challenge those aspects of anorexia that are problematic to them.

If therapists are open to the possibility that young people might value positively some aspects of an anorectic lifestyle, then the externalizing conversations that take place can become far richer. One of the reasons for this is that if therapists play a role in acknowledging what it is that people value in this lifestyle, it then becomes much easier for people to be clear about those aspects that they don't value, those aspects that are restricting them or constraining them, that are making it virtually impossible for them to make much of an appearance in life. These discernments can go hand in hand.

For some people who are struggling with anorexia, a sentiment about life as a work of beauty is very important to them. In some ways, this is akin to the idea that life can be a work of art. This is somewhat controversial to acknowledge. But for some people there is something about the aesthetics of living associated with some aspects of an anorexic lifestyle to which they are very drawn.

Through careful therapeutic conversations, it becomes possible for people to describe and to speak about those sentiments of living that they value and to which they aspire. It is possible to honor these sentiments of living and to further develop them while, at the same time, enabling people to break free of the life-threatening and highly constraining aspects of anorexia nervosa.

Why is it important to find out which sentiments of living these people value and aspire to?

Like any other therapeutic consultation, hearing about what people give value to creates a foundation for collaboration. There is no way that the lifestyle of a person is going to be totally in accordance with the life-threatening aspects of anorexia nervosa. There are always going to be expressions of life that contradict these life-threatening and constraining aspects, even if these are difficult to locate at first. It is quite critical that along with the characterization and articulation of the operations and activities of the problem, that we get to hear about some expressions of life that are not in harmony with the problem.

These alternative expressions have a foundation in what these people give value to, what they intend for their lives. And the social and relational history of what they give value to can then be traced in these therapeutic conversations. These particular skills and knowledges will have been developed in the history of their relationships with others. And so, these conversations open up the opportunity for the identification of other voices with which these people begin to feel more joined. This process of richly describing preferred storylines of identity and how these are linked to the lives of significant others is critical because it provides another territory in which people can stand, a territory freer of the constraints of anorexia nervosa.

As this process of reauthoring takes place, it often becomes possible to link some of the sentiments of life that drew the person toward an anorectic lifestyle into these alternative storylines. For instance, a person's valuing of life as a work of beauty, or as a work of art, may be taken into storylines in ways that can engender connectedness rather than isolation, self-care rather than self-possession. To trace a social and relational history of the sentiments of life that are valued by people enables them to stand in another territory of identity. This is a territory of identity from which these people can take some steps, with the support of others, to reclaim their lives from those very negative aspects of anorexia nervosa.

CHAPTER 7

The Responsibilities

WORKING WITH MEN WHO HAVE PERPETRATED VIOLENCE

*T*his *chapter outlines an approach to working with men who have perpetrated violence against women.[1] It offers an account of some of the assumptions that orient this work, provides a "map" to guide conversations with men, and includes documentation of certain aspects of these conversations.*

CONSIDERATIONS OF SAFETY AND PARTNERSHIP

At the outset, it is important to acknowledge that in working with men who have perpetrated violence against women, the first priority is to ensure the safety of women and children. Prior to engaging men in the sort of explorations described in this chapter, steps to protect the safety of women and children are undertaken. What is more, in order to continually gauge the effects of conversations with men, processes of accountability to the experiences of women and children are required (see Hall, 1994; Tamasese & Waldegrave, 1993; Tamasese, Waldegrave, Tuhaka, & Campbell, 1998; White, 1994). These considerations provide the backdrop to the approach to working with men that is outlined here.

STARTING ASSUMPTIONS

The assumptions that are outlined in this chapter are non-totalizing of men who perpetrate violence. Non-totalizing assumptions open space for men who perpetrate violence to experience an identity that it not defined by their acts of abuse, and to take responsibility for these acts of abuse. These assumptions include the following:

- The men who are referred to me for perpetrating violence are not the originators of the techniques of power they employ.
- The men who are referred to me for perpetrating violence are not the authors of the constructions of men's, women's, and children's identities that are associated with their abusive ways.

These techniques of power and constructions of identity are sponsored by the discourses of men's culture.[2] Among other things, these discourses are characterized by truth claims that are given an objective reality status and that are considered to be universal. These are truth claims about the identity of men, women, and children (e.g., about masculinity); about the nature of life and of the world (e.g., about the "nature" of the relationships of gender); and about the order of things in the world, including matters such as the rankings of importance (e.g., about the nature of men's entitlement).

These discourses of men's culture are also characterized by rules that privilege specific knowledges of men's culture, and that position the knowledges of women and children low down in the hierarchy of knowledge. These include rules about what counts as "legitimate" knowledge; who might possess this knowledge; where this knowledge is to be stored; the circumstances under which this knowledge can be expressed; and the position and location from which this knowledge can be expressed.

Accomplices and Recruits of Domination

The assumption that men who perpetrate abuse are not the originators of these techniques of power or the authors of these constructions of identity and gender leads to a perspective that they are accomplices to the projects of domination that are shaped by these discourses. This assumption also leads to the perspective that these men are recruits, and that as recruits, they have undergone an apprenticeship in these abusive ways of being.

This assumption that these men are accomplices and recruits does not diminish the acknowledgment that they are individually responsible for the acts of tyranny that they have perpetrated on the lives of others. But it does support the conclusion that it is the responsibility of men (as a community) to:

- Address abuse.
- Develop an exposé of the discourses of men's culture.
- Make reparation.
- Develop ways of being in the world and in relationships to others that are not exploitative and that are nonabusive.

The Responsibilities

Thus, when meeting with men who have perpetrated abuse, it is helpful to think about the "responsibilities." The acknowledgment of responsibility for acts of tyranny that a man has perpetrated on the lives of others, and for the consequences of these acts, is an individual responsibility. These other responsibilities are on the shoulders of men, and, in this approach, individual men who are referred for perpetrating abuse are joined by other men in taking up these responsibilities. These assumptions inform the development of an approach . . .

- That is nonshaming and that is not "other-confrontational" (i.e., an approach that features the strong confrontation of men by others, including counselors).
- In which these men are unlikely to experience their identities being totalized.
- That will set the context for men to critique their own abusive actions and ways of thinking.

THERAPIST AWARENESS OF THE TECHNIQUES, PRACTICES, AND CONSTRUCTIONS OF DOMINATION

Therapists who work with men who perpetrate abuse have learned much about . . .

- Techniques that are routinely employed by men for reducing culpability (e.g., minimization, denial, blaming, and excusing).
- Overt and covert practices of power (e.g., the reinterpretation of the subject's history and the isolation of the subject; the utilization of inconsistency; the exceptionalizing of specific individuals, including therapists; methods of intimidation; practices of evaluation of others; and so on).
- Constructions of life and gender identity that are associated with these practices of power (e.g., specific attitudes, mindsets, outlooks, viewpoints, and ways of thinking).

These learnings can be expressed in ways that make it clear that the therapist is not naïve with regard to these techniques, practices, and constructions. For example, upon being subject to practices of covert power (e.g., the exceptionalizing of the therapist—"You are the only person who can truly understand"—or the utilization of the "gaze," which inverts the focus of the therapeutic conversation), the therapist can suggest a review of what is happening within the context of the conversation that is hindering progress. For example:

> "Something interesting is happening in this conversation. Initially the focus of our discussion was on your actions, and there was a subtle inversion in this focus to the point that we are now talking about my adequacy to be of assistance to you. I have experienced this before, and have recorded this as a practice of power that is a hurdle to progress. In fact, I have developed a list of the sort of strategies that can be employed in this situation that can make it impossible for these therapeutic conversations to be of benefit. I will retrieve this list and suggest that we work through it together, as this will make it more possible for us to spot any further hurdles to the development of our work. If it is okay with you, whenever I spot such hurdles, I will suggest that we consult this list again and talk about how this hurdle might be named and circumvented. In this way, we can be investigative reporters together."

Externalizing the Techniques, Practices, and Constructions of Dominance

Another option that sets the scene for more productive conversations is to invite the externalization of these techniques, practices, and constructions. Men can be invited to refer to their experience of the world in further developing this exposé on these techniques, practices, and constructions. These are the techniques of reducing culpability, overt and covert practices of power, and constructions of life and identity associated with these practices that men have witnessed out in the world, from the local community context through to the world stage of international politics. I refer to this as "going macro." The following conversational "map" provides a guide to this process. This conversational map seeks to make it possible for men to take responsibility for actions of violence or abuse they have enacted, to take responsibility for proposals of reparation, and to mend what might be mended. The categories described here are avenues for exploration. Responsibility is the *outcome* of these explorations, not the starting point.

GOING MACRO: EXPOSÉ OF TECHNIQUES AND PRACTICES OF DOMINATION (DISTANT)

Men can be invited to refer to their experiences of the world and what they have witnessed in relation to techniques and practices of domination. "What options would be open to a man if he intended to dominate women and children? What techniques and practices of domination and coercion are available?" During this exposé, these strategies of domination are documented. This documentation includes where and when the man has witnessed these practices.

EXPOSÉ OF STRATEGIES, TECHNIQUES, PRACTICES OF ABUSE (CLOSE)

It then becomes possible to interview men about which of these techniques, practices, and constructions they have been an accomplice to, and to encourage them to identify the processes of recruitment to which they have been subject throughout the history of their lives. The documents that have been generated can be used to scaffold a conversation about whether any of the man's actions reflect being an instrument of, or accomplice to, this culture of domination. The man can be asked if he recognizes any of his own actions on this list in a minor or major sense. The degree to which he has engaged in the techniques and practices of domination can be rated, by the man, on a scale from 1 to 10. While remaining clear that the man is not the author of these technologies of power, or practices of abuse, all the actions that he has taken that represent being an accomplice to this culture are acknowledged and documented. This process is contextualizing the man's actions. This doesn't excuse them, nor does it totalize the man as an "abusive man." A man cannot take responsibility for abuse if he identifies as an "abusive man." This process is creating space for the man to start to think about how he might have been an accomplice to, or instrument of, a culture of domination.

EXPOSÉ OF CONSTRUCTS, MEANINGS, AND ATTITUDES USED TO JUSTIFY ABUSE (DISTANT)

Men can be invited to develop an exposé of the attitudes that they have witnessed being expressed in men's culture that are used to justify the abuse of others. This does not involve giving a lecture. Instead, men's own observations in relation to attitudes of male supremacy and entitlement can be elicited, providing an opportunity for these attitudes and constructs to be named, categorized, and documented.

EXPOSÉ OF CONSTRUCTS, MEANINGS, AND ATTITUDES USED TO JUSTIFY ABUSE (CLOSE)

While recognizing that this is a difficult conversation, it then becomes possible to support the man to develop an exposé of the constructs, meanings, and attitudes that he has used to justify abuse. The man is invited to identify which constructs, meanings, and attitudes he has been an instrument of, or an accomplice to.

IDENTIFICATION OF EXPERIENCES THAT RECRUITED THE MAN AS AN ACCOMPLICE/PARTICIPANT/INSTRUMENT OF THE CULTURE OF DOMINATION

The man can then be interviewed about the processes of recruitment to which he has been subject throughout his life.

"How did you get introduced to these practices of abuse? What have you seen? When did you first witness such techniques of domination? How were you recruited to act in these ways?" Throughout this process, it remains clear that the man is not the originator of these strategies, techniques, practices, constructs, meanings, and values.

MAPPING SHORT-TERM AND LONG-TERM CONSEQUENCES OF ABUSE ON ALL PARTIES AND RELATIONSHIPS (DISTANT AND CLOSE)

With the techniques and practices of domination articulated; with the constructs, meanings, and values that are used to justify abuse acknowledged; and having had some chance to identify the ways in which they have become recruits or accomplices to the culture of domination, men can then be supported in mapping the consequences of these techniques, practices, and constructions. This process can begin with speculation about the consequences of abuse in a general sense, not directly speaking about the acts the man has perpetrated. While this conversation is taking place, the therapist can listen carefully for any sign of the man attributing significance to the consequences of abuse. Most men try to diminish the significance of the effects of abuse, so if there is a moment where significance is attributed to the consequences of abuse, this provides an opportunity for further enquiry. How has he managed to attribute this significance?

Following this more general mapping of the effects of abuse, it then becomes possible to return to the macro list generated earlier, and to the techniques and practices of abuse that the man has identified being an accomplice to. The man can then be interviewed about the consequences of these practices of abuse, both short-term and long-term, on the lives of all those involved (woman, man, the relationship, any children, and so on) and their relationships.

The idea of an apology will be meaningless until significance is attributed to the consequences of abuse. Until this attribution is made, there are limited options for men to take to heal what might be healed.

IDENTIFICATION OF UNIQUE OUTCOMES/EXCEPTIONS: WHERE THE MAN "DRAWS THE LINE"

During the early stages of this conversational map, the therapist listens for any times in which the man draws a line: "I'd never do this." There is always a bottom line for men, practices in which they would not participate. When these are identified, therapists can respond with a non-normative inquiry. Rather than saying "That's good," therapists can ask, "How come? Why not? Why wouldn't you do that?" At any time, it is possible to go back to the documents that list a range of techniques of domination and ask "Why not these other techniques? How come? I'd like to understand this." This can be the starting point to scaffold conversations: "If this statement doesn't fit a culture of control, what does it fit? If you were to hear another man speak of this, what would you call it?" and so on. If there are certain strategies or attitudes to which the man has not been an accomplice, these indicate to us certain values the man holds that contradict some aspects of a culture of control/domination. These are unique outcomes. These are entry points to other territories of life.

MORE RICHLY DESCRIBING OTHER STORIES/TERRITORIES OF LIFE

The categories of inquiry described thus far contribute to the deconstruction of the discourses of men's culture. It is in the context of these conversations that men experience a degree of separation of their identity from abusive ways of being. It is in this space that points of entry to subordinate storyline development can be taken up. These points of entry are available in responses to the "why" questions of externalizing conversations, in the form of unique outcomes, or can be garnered from what is absent but implicit in these men's expressions.

At this point, it is possible to use a range of narrative practices to determine the significance of these unique outcomes, and to richly describe other storylines of identity, other territories of life. It becomes the therapist's task to more thickly describe the attitudes or practices of life that the man gives value to that don't fit with abusive practices and attitudes. There will always be a history to what a man gives values to, a history that relates in some way to another sense of being in relationships with women and children. For instance, perhaps the man witnessed something different in another family. We can proceed to trace the history of what the man accords value. These alternative values will fit with some other belief or idea about what it might be wise to do, and some other purpose or dream for life. These other values will not have come out of the blue, which is why historical inquiry is critical.

These reauthoring conversations are essential, for they provide men with an alternative territory of life and identity in which to stand and from which they can strongly critique their own abusive and exploitative actions, and in which they will begin to develop some familiarity with other ways of orienting to their relationship with others and the world. As these alternative territories of identity are further drawn in the context of reauthoring conversations, men begin to engage with and further develop relationship practices that are nonabusive and nonexploitative.

It is in the context of these reauthoring conversations that the meanings of words such as *responsibility, respect, kindness,* etc., are developed to the extent that they become concepts about life and principles of living. It is this concept development that provides the foundation for responsible action and personal agency.

WAYS FORWARD: FORMULATING PROPOSALS FOR REPARATION, TO MEND WHAT MIGHT BE MENDED

When men have an alternative territory in which to stand, it becomes possible to talk about ways of going forward. Problem solving is a sophisticated achievement. Persons have to be at a certain distance from the immediacy of their own experience in order to problem-solve. They have to be able to:

- Hypothesize or speculate on what actions are yet to happen (steps that are available to them).
- Predict other people's responses to those actions.
- Develop plans for how they might handle contingencies (e.g., discouraging responses, disqualifying or diminishing responses).

It is therefore necessary to support men in coming up with specific proposals in relation to how they might act, what reactions these actions might receive, and how they might, in turn, respond to those reactions. This process of formulating proposals for action needs to be done in a way that prioritizes women's and children's safety and that renders the man accountable to those people who have been subject to his abuse. Otherwise the man might develop proposals for actions that represent, to him, being more loving or caring in his relationship, but this doesn't necessarily mean that these actions will be experienced by others in the way that the man assumes.

There are a number of points to consider here. First, this process has, as its highest priority, the safety of women and children. Processes of accountability are required in order to ensure that the interests of women and children remain centered at all times (see Hall, 1994; Tamasese et al., 1998; Tamasese & Walde-grave, 1993; White, 1994). If women do not wish to enter into this process, it does not proceed.

Second, it is not fair to place women in the position of having to come up with proposals for men's actions. Instead, the task is for men to come up with proposals to which women can respond. If a man comes up with a proposal that doesn't work for the woman partner, it's then up to the man to go back and work on the proposal again. The responsibility should never be on women's shoulders to make proposals for men's actions.

Highly particular (not generic) proposals are required about the following:

- Ways of being in relationships
- Acts of reparation
- Acts of apology
- Different relationship acts that will ensure the safety of women and children.

This process involves talking about and making proposals of steps for the man/men to take to ensure the safety of women and children, and then consulting with the women and children about these proposals. As this process might initially be quite fraught for the partner, I often bring in other people who might represent the woman, or find others who can stand with the woman and the children in responding to these proposals. Similarly, I also often involve other men in joining to take responsibility for developing these proposals. These other men may have, in the past, separated from being an accomplice to practices of abuse, or they may be family members (grandfathers, uncles, friends of the family) who place a high value on the safety of women and children and on practices of respect.[3]

DOCUMENTATION TO ASSIST IN SEPARATING FROM AN ETHIC OF CONTROL

At this point, it is relevant to include two different forms of therapeutic documents that can be used in work with men who have perpetrated violence. The first of these involves a letter that invites men to rigorously reflect on the ways in which their actions in the course of a day have been influenced by an ethic of control or an ethic of care.[4]

Dear _____,

The following is a brief summary of some of the thoughts that came out of our conversation. They are not cast in stone, and you will probably want to modify these terms and make alterations to these lists of elements. I have put this together in response to your request for a map of your own. In drawing out these distinctions around elements of the ethic of control and the ethic of care, I am not proposing that it is possible to always engage with the ethic of care to the exclusion of the ethic of control. But it is clear from your own observations that your life has become more heavily weighted on the left-hand side of these distinctions, although you do have the ability to more significantly invest yourself in expressions of life that reflect those elements on the right-hand side. I believe that the exercise that I have proposed will help speed a re-weighting of your life and provide you with a growing sense of authenticity.

In this exercise, take a diary and rule a line down the middle of each page. On each and every day, spend an hour reflecting on the events of the day with the purpose of sorting your actions into the left- and right-hand columns. Give special attention to identifying the habits of thought and action that give rise to those elements of expression entered into the left-hand column, and to the purposes, values, beliefs, hopes, and dreams that inspire those elements of expression in the right-hand column. With this exercise, insist on absolute honesty with yourself.

Yours sincerely,
Michael White

ETHIC OF CONTROL	ETHIC OF CARE
On my terms	Trusting of others
Control of self/others as priority	Partnership/cooperation as priority
Conditioned responses	Responsiveness to others
On automatic	Spontaneity
Seen to be right	Honesty in regard to truth and personal failings
Emotionally disconnected	Emotionally connected
Sense of entitlement	Humility
The elements that make up this ethic of control are founded on certain habits of thought and action. These habits of thought and action can be quite intoxicating and toxic. Giving one's life over to these habits renders one's life an instrument of the ethic of control.	The elements that make up this ethic of care are founded on integrity and on certain skills of relationship that open space for one's own life and for the lives of others. Engaging with this ethic contributes to the development of a congruence of preferred purposes, values, beliefs, hopes, and dreams, on the one hand, and one's actions, on the other hand.

DOCUMENTING RICH STORY DEVELOPMENT

Documentation can also play a part in the rich development of subordinate storylines. I do not believe that we have attended to even 50% of the task of working with men who have perpetrated violence if we have not fostered the rich development of subordinate storylines of these men's lives. As men start to experience a degree of separation of their identity from abusive ways of being, reauthoring conversations can begin. As mentioned above, these conversations trace the histories of certain values a man holds that contradict some aspects of a culture of control/domination. It is the context of this historical inquiry that words such as *friendship, loyalty, honesty, kindness,* and *caring* are developed into concepts about life and principles of living. And as mentioned before, it is this concept development that provides the foundation for men to take action to redress the harms they have done and to heal what can be healed.

The letter below was written to follow up a conversation that took place in a maximum security men's prison in Sydney in a special antiviolence unit. All the men in this unit have histories of perpetrating significant violence. They have all also volunteered to attend the unit. The head psychologist, Rachael Haggett, invited me and David Denborough to visit the unit and conduct a series of interviews. The following letter recaps a reauthoring conversation that linked Anthony's current efforts to turn things around in his life to a number of significant friendships and relationships. The letter also summarizes the reflections offered by an outsider-witness group who responded to the interview.

> *Dear Anthony,*
>
> *It was great to meet with you yesterday and to be introduced, through our conversation, to your friend David, your grandfather, and your mother Susan. This letter is just a chance to recap some of the stories that you spoke about so that there can be a written record of these.*
>
> *Anthony, you spoke so clearly about how your current efforts to turn things around in your life are linked to your friendship with David. You described how his death affected you and that this is contributing to your determination to make changes in your life. You spoke about how you don't want to see your friends getting hurt.*

We heard about your childhood friendship with David. You spoke about your soccer-playing days together and your love of sport, and we could just picture the two of you out on the field together. You described David as "full of life, with a good heart." It sounds like he was also very funny and that his humor really added something to your life. You described what your connection with David stood for in your life— "friendship, loyalty, honesty, kindness, and caring."

It wasn't just the good times that you shared. You spoke about how you and David had something in common in relation to your stepfathers. You spoke about how your stepfather was "very cold to me," and it sounds like this was also true for David.

Then, when David's mother was imprisoned, he came to live with you. You shared your clothes with him. You said: "He could lean on me." And, "If I was feeling down he'd play a part in lifting me up." You described the times when you would sit outside the prison waiting for him after he had visited his mum. And we wondered what it might have meant for David to have you there for him at these times. We heard how you became brothers to each other.

You also described how David was close to your mother, Susan. And how, since you were in prison, he would take Susan shopping. It sounded like not only were you brothers to each other, but that David also became a son to your mother.

We then came to hear about your grandfather, who sounded like a very interesting and kind man. You described how he would take you and David to soccer, how he spoke eight languages, and how he would give you quizzes in all sorts of things. If you got the answer right, he would say, "Spot on, kid."

Anthony, you spoke about how you were not violent during these years, that you were quiet, you worked hard, and loved sports and your friendship with David. You described how when David was around, you weren't in trouble.

We heard that things started to go wrong after your grandfather's death. That around the same time you got into a relationship with a girl who was using drugs and that you started using too. You spoke about how "I was 15 then and that's when things started going downhill."

It was from then on that violence became part of your life. During this time, you said that David was always trying to "get me to wake up." He used to visit you in prison, and he was always valuing your life.

When David was killed, it sounds like you were at a crossroads. When your grandfather died, when you were 15, things "started going downhill." But when David was killed, it sounds like you took a different path, like there was a legacy from your grandfather and from David that you picked up. One of the psychologists who was listening said that it sounded like you had found a precious stone or an heirloom that you started to polish, that you started to treasure. And that this is why you are working so hard in the unit, trying to make changes.

You spoke about how you are now trying to get back into your life those things that were there when you were younger— the "friendship, loyalty, honesty, kindness, and caring" that you had with David.

You said, "I want to do this for my mum." You said that your mum had been through so much, that you had put her through so much, but that she has already begun seeing the changes that you are making. "She has seen a lot of changes," you said. And that "she's got hope that I've woken up to myself."

Toward the end of the conversation, it was like David and your grandfather and Susan were somehow with us in the room. You said that if David were there, he'd probably say, "About time you snapped out of it!" You said that he'd be happy. You said that your grandfather would probably say, "Spot on, kid." You said, "He'd feel proud, how he used to feel about me." You told us something else that your grandfather used to say to you: "When you are trying to do something difficult, think about it, take your time, and do it properly."

After you listened to the reflections from the team, you said that a number of things stood out for you:

- *"The comraderie of my early friendship with David"*
- *"The warmth" that was described by one of the team*
- *"How one team member could relate because they also didn't have a father"*

- *"How they acknowledged the pain"*
- *"The image of the precious rock"*
- *"It meant a lot to me that they got emotional. Their understanding makes a difference. It means I will work harder."*

You talked about how you will take this experience away with you.

We have also taken away our experience of meeting with you, Anthony. Thanks again for introducing us to David, your grandfather, and Susan. And we hope to see you again later in the year.

Warm regards,
Michael White and David Denborough

This letter documents a one-off interview. I have included it here not because it is an example of long-term effective work, but because it illustrates the possibilities of this practice. It describes the sort of reauthoring process that can more richly describe stories/territories of life that can then provide the foundation for the formulation of proposals for reparation, to mend what might be mended, and to prevent further harm.

THE RESPONSIBILITIES OF MEN TO ADDRESS VIOLENCE

This chapter has outlined an approach to working with men who have perpetrated violence. Within this approach, violence is not viewed as an aberration but as intimately linked to the discourses of men's culture. This observation underscores the importance of men's responsibility to address this violence— the importance of this being on the shoulders of *men*, rather than on the shoulders of an individual man.

On account of this perspective, it is routine to invite other men to join this work, men who could be considered "alumni."

These are men who have volunteered to join me in my work with other men who are following in their footsteps, in addressing the abuses of men's culture. Men with insider knowledge of these abusive ways are well positioned to contribute to the exposé of techniques employed for reducing culpability, of overt and covert practices of power, and of those constructions of life and of gender identity that privilege domination. These men have a dual role: They contribute significantly to the development of an exposé of the discourses of men's culture that inform actions that are abusive, and they also participate as outsider-witnesses in contributing to the development of the subordinate storylines of the man's life.

These outsider-witness retellings are vital in the repositioning of men who perpetrate abuse. Among other things, this is a repositioning from which it becomes possible for these men to become interested in how they've been an instrument of men's culture and to find ways to challenge this. It is in this context that dominant discourses of men's culture are deconstructed, and in which men experience a degree of separation of their identity from abusive ways of being. As men begin to experience this separation and to step into different territories of identity, it becomes increasingly possible to strongly critique their own abusive actions and to initiate reparation.

EDITOR'S NOTES

1. This chapter limits its scope to describing an approach to working with heterosexual men in relation to violence against their women partners. The paper does not consider same-sex or transgender experience, nor does it seek to deconstruct the terms "man" and "men." It also does

not engage with considerations of cultural difference. For discussion about some of these concerns see Yuen & White (2007).

2. For more descriptions of what is meant by "men's culture," see White (1992).

3. For a detailed example of involving other men in this process, see White (2001).

4. Michael drew upon the work of Sharon Welch (1990) in these descriptions of the ethic of control and the ethic of care.

CHAPTER 8

Externalizing and Responsibility

I think it's possible to develop externalizing conversations that increase a sense of responsibility, or develop a sense of responsibility, rather than diminish it. And I think the important point is that it's not the externalizing itself that enables this, it's what happens next. In one of my presentations, I refer to a conversation with a young man who was in lots of trouble, which was strongly linked to his acts of violence. He was violent to his younger siblings, he was assaulting his mother, he attempted to assault his father, and he was in trouble at school for violence. Everybody was quite at their wits' end over this situation, so the only family member who would accompany him to speak with me was his mother. What follows is a brief account of that conversation.

His mother talks a lot about her frustration, her anguish, and her sense of failure as a mother. She also speaks about experiences of being assaulted by this young man and the consequences on her life. She speaks of her desperation and of her sorrow at facing the possibility of fostering out her son. He's very much a passenger in the conversation. Even when she's crying, I see that he's not very engaged. When I turn to him and attempt to engage him in the conversation, he's not very present in it. This young man is considered to be "lacking in insight" and irresponsible. He rarely speaks to adults, so I feel grateful for even one-word responses.

My understanding is that responsibility itself is a *concept*; it's not just a word, it's a concept. Now this young man knows the word, but that's all it is. For him, the meaning of that word is not developed in any way. My understanding is that, without the development of that word as a concept, he won't have a foundation for taking what would be considered responsible action. For men who are referred to me for perpetrating abuse, they know the word *respect* but it's only a word—it's not a concept about life or about identity.

I think one of the things about these externalizing conversations is that they do open up possibilities for the development of these concepts. I decide that it might be helpful to actually interview him about the effects of this violence on his own life. And so, I want him to name it. What name would he give to this? He calls it "the hurting"— he hurts others, so he calls it "the hurting"—and I get him to characterize "the hurting" a bit more. I'm interested in the effects of "the hurting," and when I inquire about this for the first time, he links "the hurting" to being split off from the family. This is an achievement—this is not just something that happens—he's actually bringing some of these events of his life into some chain of association. For him to actually link "the hurting" to certain consequences in his own life is an achievement, and we linger in that conversation for some time.

Then I want to know how he feels about his situation, so I consult him about his experience with "the hurting" and its consequences. From our previous conversation, he now has a *reflecting surface*—he has something on which to reflect. Well, he's not too happy about this; he says, "I mind this." I ask, "What do you mean?" He tells me he means that it's not okay, he's not happy with it. I want to know why that is, and he says he doesn't know, he can't answer the question. All he can say is that "I don't want a life like my sister, and that's why I mind." He has a 16-year-old sister who's living in a small flat with an older adult male as her partner and two male friends of this man. And I say, "Well, okay, I understand that you mind because you wouldn't like a life like your sister, but that doesn't tell me why you mind being split off from your family. I don't understand this," and he gives me permission to consult his mother. When I ask her, she says, "Well, maybe it's because of what he's missing out on." I ask, "Well, what is that?" and she says, "Belonging." I then turn to him and I ask, "Does that fit for you?," and he says, "Belonging," and I ask, "Well, what do you mean 'belonging'?" These questions are playing a role in the development of these concepts.

At another point in the conversation, I ask him a little bit about how this "hurting" affects how he feels, because I can see his mother's crying. So I ask, "Well, how does it have you feeling? Does it make you sad?" He's not sure. We talk a bit more, and he says that it does make him sad. I ask, "Well, does this show itself like it shows itself in your mother? Like with tears, or in a different way?" He says, "Different way." And I ask, "Well, I can see where it is in her body; where is it in your body? Is it here, or there, or there? Where is it?" He chooses the heart out of a range of choices. Then I ask, "What's it like when you're feeling that sadness in your heart?" and he says, "I feel all alone at this time." Now, he's never given voice to these understandings about life; this is entirely new. So, once again, this is an achievement: He's linking these acts of violence to "hurting," to sadness, to where that touches him in his body, to being all alone in life—and these are all new developments.

Now, there's some assumption that this young man should be responsible for his actions. But he has no foundation for that yet—remember, responsibility is a *concept*, it's not just a word. So I then ask "What's this like for you?" I get him to reflect on these experiences, and he tells me that this is really something that he's uncomfortable about. Again, I can ask, "Why? Could you help me understand that?" He comes up with another concept about life in response—I learn that "the hurting" allies itself with the anger and is taking control of his life. He'd never expressed this before. How does he feel about that? He says, "Well, I'd like to be able to do something about the shape of my own life." He doesn't use these words, exactly, but something like that. Now, *that's* responsibility, isn't it? I ask him what he means by that, and gradually he comes to the word *responsibility*. And so we explore that further, and *responsibility* actually becomes a concept for him.

I think that through externalizing conversations, people bring their actions into relationship with consequences. They then reflect on their experience of that, and in response, come up with conclusions, or give voice to certain learnings about life that are abstracted from the exact situation. The reason I am stressing concept development is that I think it's the development of these concepts that makes it possible for people to do what we call "taking responsibility." Put simply, the steps are (1) externalizing the problem; (2) reviewing the consequences; (3) reflecting on the consequences and then asking about the "why" of those reflections; (4) coming up with conclusions about one's own life, or about what one wants, or about what one gives value to, or about what one intends for one's life; and (5) then taking that up in further word development so it becomes a concept, split off from the concrete situation. In this particular interview, this boy says that, among other things, the hurting is "borrowing" his belonging. I know that "belonging" is now split off from the concrete circumstances; it's become an abstract idea or a concept about life. I hope this brief account helps to show how externalizing conversations open possibilities for people to take responsibility for their lives.

CHAPTER 9

Revaluation and Resonance

NARRATIVE RESPONSES TO TRAUMATIC EXPERIENCE

This chapter explores the significance of revaluation and resonance in addressing experiences of trauma and reinvigorating the "stream of consciousness" or language of inner life. To quote William James (1890) on the "stream of consciousness":

> Like a bird's life, it seems to be made of an alternation of flights and perchings. The rhythm of language expresses this, where every thought is expressed in a sentence, and every sentence closed by a period. The resting places are usually occupied by sensorial imaginations of some sort, whose peculiarity is that they can be held before the mind for an indefinite time, and contemplated without changing; the places of flight are filled with thoughts of relations, static or dynamic, that for the most part obtain between the matters contemplated in the periods of comparative rest. (p. 243)

It is invariably the case that efforts to directly address people's experiences of trauma are unproductive at best, and, in many circumstances, deleterious. Such efforts can contribute to experiences of retraumatization and to a sense of alienation. To engage in efforts to directly contradict and destabilize the negative conclusions about a person's identity that are generated in the context of trauma, conclusions that are stored in the semantic memory system and that have the status of fact, can contribute to a sense of alienation, of being disrespected, and even to an experience of being mocked.

The primary therapeutic task in addressing the effects of trauma on people's lives is then to provide a context for the development or redevelopment of the sort of personal reality that gives rise to the sense of self that is referred to as "myself." This is the sense of self that is associated with the internalization of a language of experience that is narrative in form and that characterizes what William James called the "stream of consciousness."

This development or redevelopment of this sense of an inner life can be achieved through a therapeutic inquiry that brings together a person's diverse experiences of life into a storyline that is unifying of these experiences and that provides a sense of personal continuity through the course of his or her history. The arrangement of life experiences around specific themes and relevant metaphors contributes significantly to this unification and sense of continuity.

In the following discussion, I address just a few of the many options that can contribute to a context for the development and revitalization of this "stream of consciousness." These options are informed by the notions of revaluation and resonance.

REVALUATION AND RESONANCE

Therapeutic inquiry is directed to the identification of those aspects of life to which people have accorded value. These might be specific purposes for one's life that are cherished; prized values and beliefs with regard to acceptance, justice, and fairness; treasured aspirations, hopes, and dreams; personal pledges, vows, and commitments to ways of being in life; special memories, images, and fantasies about life that are linked to significant themes; metaphors that represent special realms of existence; and so on. In the context of therapeutic conversations, these aspects of people's lives can be identified and revalued through a range of resonant responses.

It is not always easy to identify these aspects of life to which people have allocated value—they have often been secreted away in places where they are safe from further ridicule and diminishment—and even when identified, it can be quite a task for people to name them. However, despite any initial difficulties that may be experienced in identifying those aspects of life to which people accord value, I believe that these are ever-present in people's expressions of living. I believe this to be so even when these people are regularly experiencing life through the thrall of dissociated traumatic memories—even at this time, there is some principle operating in the selection of memories. The fact of the existence of these aspects of life that are accorded value is, in itself, an extraordinary tribute to the person's refusal to relinquish or to be separated from what was so powerfully disrespected and demeaned in the context of trauma.

The notion of the "absent but implicit" is highly significant as a guide to us in this work. Although this chapter does not afford the opportunity for a thorough review of this notion, I will present some hypotheses about the sort of psychological pain and emotional distress that is experienced in the context of impinging traumatic memories. These hypotheses are founded on the notion of the "absent but implicit."

Ongoing psychological pain in response to trauma in people's lives might be considered a testimony to the significance of what it was that those individuals held precious that was violated through the experience of trauma. This can include people's understandings about:

- Cherished purposes for one's life
- Prized values and beliefs around acceptance, justice, and fairness
- Treasured aspirations, hopes, and dreams
- Moral visions about how things might be in the world
- Significant pledges, vows, and commitments about ways of being in life.

If psychological pain can be considered to be a testimony to such purposes, values, beliefs, aspirations, hopes, dreams, moral visions, and commitments, then the experienced intensity of this pain can be considered to be a reflection of the degree to which these intentional states were held precious by persons.

Day-to-day emotional distress in response to trauma in people's histories might be considered a tribute to individuals' ability to maintain a constant relationship with all of those purposes, values, beliefs, aspirations, hopes, dreams, visions, and commitments held precious—to their refusal to relinquish or to be separated from that which was so powerfully disrespected and demeaned in the context of trauma, from that which they continue to revere.

Psychological pain and emotional distress might be understood to be elements of a legacy expressed by people who, in the face of the nonresponsiveness of the world around them, remain resolute in their determination that the trauma that they and others have gone through will not be for nothing—that things must change on account of what they have gone through. Once identified, whatever it is about their life that the person has accorded value provides an orientation for the development of resonance within the therapeutic conversation. In the following discussion, I present just some of the therapeutic options for the development of this resonance.

Resonance #1: To What Is Accorded Value

Initial resonance can be achieved in the therapist's responses to what has been accorded value, responses that:

- Contribute to a heightened curiosity about and acknowledgment of this aspect of the person's life.
- Provide a scaffold for the attribution of preferred meaning to these aspects of a person's life.
- Load these aspects of the person's life with significance.

These therapist responses are resonant in that they have the effect of re-presenting, to the person, that which is treasured.

Apart from providing a starting point for the redevelopment and revitalization of the language of inner life associated with the stream of consciousness, these therapist responses build a foundation for the development of a sense of mutual understanding and familiarity that can have an immediate effect in turning back some of the effects of trauma. For it is in this resonance that a person recognizes his or her "self." It is this resonance that contributes to the reinstatement of an "I" in relation to "myself." It is in contributing to the development of this resonance that the therapist initiates a reproduction of the sort of context that gives rise to symbolic play and play with symbols within the therapeutic conversation.

Resonance #2: Reverberations Through Time

The introduction of therapeutic responses that contribute to experiences of resonance in the external world provides a foundation for the development of the sort of internal resonances that displace a linear world of "one damned thing after another" and that introduce complexity into a person's sense of their life. The resonance that is set off by these therapist-initiated responses to what a person accords value has the effect of evoking positive images of life and identity that often present to the person in metaphorical and visual forms. As these images build in these conversations, they have the potential to set off reverberations into the history of the person's experiences of life. At this time, the therapist can introduce an inquiry that identifies the way in which these reverberations touch on memories that are resonant with these images of the present.

These memories that are resonant with the images of the present are like the "perchings" referred to by William James in his account of the stream of consciousness. It is in the linking of episodes of life through history that is provided by these resonances that new connections and patterns of experience are developed, and that unifying themes of life are identified and named through metaphor. This process sponsors the development of an inner world that can be visualized, and a sense of aliveness that displaces a sense of emptiness and deadness.

Resonance #3: Themes of Life and Intentional-State Understandings

As the sense of an inner personal reality is built in the context of this therapeutic inquiry, people not only experience the development of an inner conversation in which otherwise singular, disparate, and discontinuous aspects of their experience become linked across time, but they also begin to experience a resonance between this linking and specific themes of life. And, more than this, a resonance develops between this linking of otherwise singular, disparate, and discontinuous aspects of experience, these themes of life, and specific intentional-state notions of life. These intentional-state notions include specific purposes, plans, and goals. At this point therapist-initiated inquiry can contribute to the acknowledgment of these intentional-state notions of life and to their rich description.

Resonance #4: The Development of "My World"

In response to this development, therapeutic conversations can provide a scaffold that brings into focus a range of events in the world that resonate with these themes and with these intentional-state understandings. For example, the therapist can invite considerations of various recent events of the person's life that might reflect these themes and intentional-state notions of life.

Once resonance is established between the significant themes of life and internal-state notions, on the one hand, and specific recent events of the person's life, on the other, the person develops a stronger sense of continuity between inner and outer worlds, between aspects of personal reality and outer reality. This experience of continuity builds a sense of a world that is in part responsive to one's existence, and sponsors a sense of personal agency. This development gives rise to new feelings of well-being and pleasure.

Resonance #5: Retelling

Another resonance is achieved through the introduction of an audience to these conversations, whose task it is to re-present, through retellings, those aspects of life to which the person accords value. Following Myerhoff (1980; 1982; 1986), I refer to this audience as an outsider-witness group. It is the task of outsider-witnesses to engage with each other in a retelling of what they witnessed and heard in the conversation between the therapist and the persons seeking consultation.

These retellings of the outsider-witnesses are not a recounting of the content of what was witnessed and heard in the tellings of the therapeutic conversation, but consist of responses to what it was about these tellings that captured their imagination and that fired their curiosity. Apart from re-presenting these particularities of the telling, outsider-witnesses provide an account of the images of life and identity that were triggered by these expressions. Further, it is the task of outsider-witnesses to embody their interest in the person's life by speaking to their understanding of why they were drawn to the expressions that they are re-presenting in their retellings—by speaking to the resonances that these expressions set off in their personal histories.

Lastly, it is the task of outsider-witnesses to provide an account of how these tellings and retellings have transported them and contributed to:

- Developments in their own sense of self
- Understandings of their own lives
- Possibilities for action in their own worlds

In stepping into this task, outsider-witnesses acknowledge the extent to which, on account of witnessing the person's expressions, they have become other than who they were at the outset of the tellings. That is, in performing this task, outsider-witnesses assume a responsibility for acknowledging the ways in which they have been transported by these expressions.

These re-presentations of outsider-witnesses are the outcome of sensitive and imaginative attunement to what might be accorded value in the person's life. When outsider-witnesses succeed in resonant responses, the person experiences a special harmony between inner and outer worlds that has been so elusive to him or her, one that provides a basis for the development of interpersonal familiarity and for a sense of mutual understanding. It is this sense of mutual understanding that is the hallmark of relating intimately to others.

Responses of admiration that construct heroic accounts of the person's life and achievements are not characteristic of the class of outsider-witness response that contributes to powerful resonances. Neither are what I have elsewhere referred to as the "practices of the applause"—congratulatory responses, giving affirmations, pointing out positives, and so on. Not only is it highly unlikely that such responses will establish resonances with what it is about life that the person has accorded value, but these responses can be experienced as controlling and alienating, and, at times, even mocking.

Resonance #6: Not for Nothing

In acknowledging transport, at times outsider-witnesses provide accounts of possible action that might be taken by them in other worlds—action that could in some way contribute to addressing injustices that others are experiencing, or that could provide some sense of redress in regard to injustices previously experienced by others. When these outsider-witnesses take steps to follow through with these actions and to ensure that the person receives feedback about these steps and their outcome, this can also set up a powerful resonance. This is a resonance between such action and what might be a person's:

- Longing for the world to be different on account of what he or she has been through.
- Secret hope that all that he or she has endured wasn't for nothing.
- Hidden desire to contribute to the lives of others who have had similar experiences.
- Fantasy about playing some part in relieving the suffering of others.
- Passion to play some part in acts of redress in relation to the injustices of the world.

This resonance between an individual's longings, hopes, desires, and fantasies and the actions taken by outsider-witnesses further strengthens the sense of continuity between inner and outer worlds, between aspects of personal reality and outer reality. As previously mentioned, this builds a sense of a world that is at least in part responsive to one's existence, sponsors the development of a sense of personal agency, and gives rise to new feelings of well-being and pleasure.

Resonance #7: Responses to Trauma

The experience of trauma is irreconcilable with themes about life that are cherished, and with preferred accounts of one's identity. Therefore, the meanings that people give to their experiences of abuse within the context of trauma invariably include powerfully negative conclusions about their identity.

Despite this, people are not passive recipients of trauma; they respond to trauma in the best way that they know how. These responses are usually consistent with accounts of identity that are associated with autobiographical memory and with the sense of self that is associated with the language of inner life. However, these responses are rarely acknowledged and appreciated within the context of trauma; instead, they are often dishonored, ridiculed, and diminished. Because of this, and because of the powerfully negative conclusions about identity that are generated in traumatic contexts, these responses to trauma are lost to memory.

However, it is possible to resurrect an account of the person's response to trauma. There are several ways in which this can be done, but it is usually achieved though imaginative and speculative projection of the revitalized sense of "myself" through the territories of trauma in one's history. For example, the skills that are performed in, and the purposes that are evident in, recent responses to relatively minor predicaments and dilemmas can become more richly known in the context of therapeutic conversations. These skills and purposes can provide a foundation for the imaginative and speculative projection to which I am referring. In this way, resonance is established between the cherished themes and preferred accounts of one's identity, on the one hand, and one's responses to trauma, on the other.

To summarize, the reconstruction and resurrection of a person's responses to trauma can significantly contribute to a regeneration and revitalization of the sense of "myself" that is a feature of the stream of consciousness. When the sense of "self" within the context of traumatic experience is rendered continuous with the sense of "myself" associated with the stream of consciousness, and when there is an account of one's responses to trauma that fits with cherished themes of one's life and with preferred accounts of one's identity, the outcome is a degree of erosion of those highly negative identity conclusions generated in the context of the trauma—an erosion of those "hardwired" disabling facts about one's life that are stored in semantic memory. As well, when the sense of "self" within the context of the traumatic experience is in some ways rendered continuous with this sense of "myself," this creates the possibility for the integration of traumatic memories into the narrative structure that is a feature of the experience of inner life.

It is through these explorations that people are able to turn traumatic memories into the same material of which their narrative of self is made. It is in the context of these explorations that traumatic memories are incorporated into the storylines of personal history in a way that validates and reinforces a sense of "myself." It is with this development that these memories are assigned beginnings and endings and relegated to history.

CLOSING THOUGHTS

In this chapter I have referenced therapeutic practice to William James's metaphor of the "stream of consciousness." I have proposed that as the language of inner life—one that is narrative in structure and that is a characteristic of this stream of consciousness—is redeveloped and revitalized, persons become less vulnerable to the phenomenon of dissociation. We can employ other metaphors to extend on our understanding of the effects of this therapeutic practice. For example, geographical metaphors can be cross-referenced with those metaphors of narrative. We might then propose that it is through the development of resonance that therapeutic conversations build what at first are islands of safety in people's lives. In the further development of these conversations, these islands become archipelagos, and eventually continents. On account of this, people find that they have other territories in which to stand as they begin to review their experiences of trauma. This contributes to new options for people to bring memories of trauma into consciousness in ways that mitigate retraumatization, in ways that provide for an integration of these traumatic memories that render them less vulnerable to dissociation.

In my work with people in addressing the effects of trauma, invariably I engage in practices of the written word. For example, I record in writing the resonances of therapeutic conversations, including those outsider-witness responses that appear most significant to the people who consult me. The outcome of this recording is a document that reflects the structure of the language of inner life: It is rich in association, metaphor, and analogy and provides persons with a ready source for recuperating the sense of "I" in relation to "myself" whenever the going is difficult.

As well as this, I routinely join with the people who consult me in the development of autobiographical documents. These are different in form and language—they are formal, authoritative, and feature claims of veracity. These documents bolster the sense of "me" and are derived in conversations distinct from those that are tailored to resonant responses and that I have described in this chapter—but that is another story.

CHAPTER 10

Engagements with Suicide

Much has been written about working with people who are suicidal. This chapter is not about this, but about working with the friends, family, neighbors, and acquaintances of those who take their lives. This chapter is about addressing the cloak of silence around the wilful acts of taking one's life. Over many years, I have been consulted by many people who have lost a friend or a relative to suicide. Usually this person who has taken his or her own life has become invisible. People find it difficult to make mention of them. The details of their lives are cloaked in silence. Very often the suicide has become a mark of shame. Suicide is totalized, despite the fact that it is a decision taken in a wide range of contexts, and it is the outcome of a universe of considerations. There is rarely an honoring of the meanings in which the person who took his or her life was engaging. To honor these meanings is not to celebrate suicide. It is not to break from a lament for things to have been different. It is not to resign oneself to the idea that the act was necessary. It is not to step back from efforts to attend to the politics of living so that people's choices might be widened. Instead, the task can be to convene honoring ceremonies that are two-sided.

While honoring the loss of the person, these ceremonies

investigate the insider meanings of suicide as these are routinely dishonored. They explore how it was possible for the person to commit suicide. What (values, skills, etc.) did it require? What kind of decision would this have been to make? This process involves rendering the suicide mindful.

Significantly, these ceremonies can explore whether the suicide was founded, in any way, on what the person gave value to throughout their life. Were they a person who, in the past, had been able to make really powerful decisions and follow through on them? By asking questions about what the suicide required (values, skills, etc.) and linking this to what was known about the person, and what linked them to others, it becomes possible to make the suicide continuous with what is known about the person. It makes it possible for participants in the ceremony to be sad for the person's struggles whilst retaining an awareness of what their existence stood for. Significantly, this can make it possible for loved ones to still feel linked with the person who has died. The following transcript conveys this process. It involves Wendy speaking about her son Ted, who committed suicide.

WENDY: It was just, just so terrible. And when I think back to the little child he was, then I think of that bright, happy little boy who then had to suffer all of this. So that's painful. And if I think about the cancer and the terrible treatment and how brave he was, that's horrible to think about. And if I think about him being into drugs, that's terrible to think about. This burden of pain that he was carrying, and then killing himself. That's horrible too. So it feels like I don't have anywhere to go.

MICHAEL: Yeah. And you have a sense that it's been something that you need to talk about for a while?

WENDY: Well, the only way I've coped with it is by just blocking it out more and more. And I've done better about not thinking about it. But of course the pitfall with that is that I've lost a sense of connection with him. And I don't want to do that. I feel that that's disloyal to him, which I don't want to do.

MICHAEL: Yeah.

WENDY: Because most of the time he was a very loving son, but, also, I would like to be able to have a sense of connection, which I've lost, in the sense that he's dead. I don't want to lose all the years that I had with him too. So I just seem to be getting nowhere.

MICHAEL: How's that affected your life—to lose that sense of connection? What's your experience of that?

WENDY: It's a great sense of emptiness for me.

MICHAEL: Emptiness. . . .

WENDY: And, of course, as a parent you have plans for the future, about what your future's going to be like with your child. You want to see him grow up and be happy and all those sorts of things. Of course, that's all gone.

MICHAEL: Yeah. . . .

WENDY: And, I guess, I feel like there was so much difficulty in our relationship even before he died. I just had already lost touch with him. If we hadn't had any of the earlier problems, and he had died in an automobile accident or something, that would have been terrible, but at least up until that time he would have been happy. You know, I could have remembered that, but now I just feel like all that effort that I put in doesn't seem to have been enough. And, so, I guess because I've also lost touch with him, his suicide increases my sense of failure.

MICHAEL: So, a sense of failure is part of the outcome for you?

WENDY: Well, I think so. I mean, logically I know I couldn't have done any more with him than I did. I got him in touch with the professionals whose help he needed. As a parent you can't be a therapist to your child. So I tried to get to get him in touch with people, and I just tried to be a good parent to him. But I don't even know what to connect back with.

MICHAEL: Yeah. What else is part of the legacy just for you at the moment? Like you said, there's the sense of emptiness, the sense of failure.

WENDY: Well, I think the loss of the future. He often used to say, "I'm pretty close to my mother." He lived away from home, but we were emotionally close. And I anticipated that we'd get over the cancer, and then we'd share a positive future. So I guess the future became even more important because of all the problems that were in the past.

MICHAEL: Yeah. . . .

WENDY: It was something that I really held on to. And I guess because of his illness I spent so much time helping him, and in lots of practical senses, like taking him to doctors' appointments, looking after him when he was in bed, getting him to the hospital, and all that sort of stuff, which meant that a lot of normal activities didn't happen. So I guess it's hard for me to think of him without thinking of taking care of him.

MICHAEL: [*Writing*] It's hard for you to think of him without thinking of taking care of him.

WENDY: And I still want to go take care of him now. So I guess that limits what I can do. Or it seems to me my options are limited.

MICHAEL: Can you help me understand a little bit about how your son's suicide has contributed to your conclusions about being a failure? I'd like to understand your interpretation of his suicide and how you would make that link.

WENDY: He experienced so much suffering, and I feel I couldn't help him enough with that pain that he could live. I don't think, given the circumstances, if I had prevented the suicide, there would have been another time. So it is the sense of not being able . . . that I couldn't help him enough.

MICHAEL: [*Writing*] To help him with his pain. So that's it, and somehow that thought cast a shadow over all of the caring that you did through those years? Is that right? Somehow casts a shadow over that?

WENDY: Seems to make it all pointless.

MICHAEL: It was all pointless?

WENDY: Well, I mean, I just feel like it was all pointless.

MICHAEL: Yeah.

WENDY: And he physically lived through having cancer, but he was so miserable that he ended up killing himself. So what was the point of all I tried to do during those years?

MICHAEL: I'm just wondering how he actually killed himself. I don't mean the mechanics of it, but how he actually achieved that. Do you know what I mean? That's a huge decision to make, and it's one that he did in the year of his life in which he was relatively clear?

WENDY: Oh, yeah, he was clear about it. My first thought when I found him, was, "Maybe he had counted on me rescuing him," 'cause he knew I was coming up that day. But in subsequently talking to people, friends of his said, "I can't understand it. He seemed so happy over the weekend and was going 'round and talking to people, and seemed to be having a good time." Which made me feel better, because I knew then that he had, in fact, really made up his mind and that's probably why he was happier and going around. So it wasn't as though it was an impulse that he thought I would probably save him from.

MICHAEL: Yeah.

WENDY: I found him on Thursday morning. Someone came

by on the Wednesday afternoon, and he'd just apparently taken the tablets. He said he was really hungry and could the friend go out and get him something to eat, which the friend did. But he also said, "Oh I'm just tired. I just really need to sleep." So at that point, he could have changed his mind and survived.

MICHAEL: Yeah, wow.

WENDY: So he was, he was totally determined and had . . .

MICHAEL: So he quit, he quit life? Yeah? Wow.

WENDY: And, you know, he did have a lot of pain in him. I just thought if he could live through the next couple of years, it might turn around and then he might be getting more positive.

MICHAEL: Yeah. Was he a person who, in the past, had been able to make really powerful decisions and follow them through in this way? Or is this the first powerful . . .

WENDY: Well, he had to be determined to—I think any child who goes though chemotherapy and surgery has to be really powerful. While he was dependent and needed reassurance, he also asked a lot of questions of the doctors and so on, whereas a lot of kids that he knew didn't.

MICHAEL: So, he was really looking at facing the truth about his condition, that and the questions and so on, and he wouldn't turn away from that?

WENDY: And I think he was just on that turning point of being that bit older.

MICHAEL: It doesn't surprise you in a way to just reflect on the power and determination of that decision?

WENDY: No.

MICHAEL: And his, what would you say, *courage*, in following through? Or, what would you say, of his . . .

WENDY: I think it was, I don't know, I guess it was courage in a way. I think he thought had he lived that things would have been worse for him.

MICHAEL: Yeah.

WENDY: And I think he felt that he'd let us down by some of the things he'd done. We'd said to him, "That's not true, we don't blame you for getting into drugs, and we don't expect you to give them up a hundred percent and never try them again." And we tried to help him feel he wasn't letting us down. But I think he believed that he was.

MICHAEL: Yeah.

WENDY: I wish I could've convinced him that he wasn't.

MICHAEL: So he was obviously concerned for his sister, and concerned for you as well, that he was letting you down in some way?

WENDY: I think so. I think he felt that he had let everyone down, 'cause I'm a fairly conventional sort of person, I suppose, and so is his sister. And I guess he had probably done some things that he didn't like either.

MICHAEL: Yeah.

WENDY: And so he felt he'd let himself down as well.

MICHAEL: Yeah.

WENDY: And . . .

MICHAEL: That he'd gone against some values that were important to him?

WENDY: I think so.

MICHAEL: Yeah.

WENDY: And yet with the pain and pressure he was under, maybe he felt he couldn't change that. He couldn't live a different life maybe.

MICHAEL: Yeah.

WENDY: I think he'd given it a pretty good shot that last year.

MICHAEL: So, he gave it a pretty good shot the last year, and then reached the conclusion, "Well, this isn't enough, and I'm going to refuse life." "A good shot" . . . you know, he kept on trying through the cancer and through a whole lot of other experiences as well. He gave it a good shot; I'm just wondering whether or not his decision to end his life has been respected in those sorts of terms by anyone?

WENDY: Well, it's respected by me, although it makes me very sad.

MICHAEL: Yeah.

WENDY: I mean, it was a very definite, active decision on his part.

MICHAEL: Yeah.

WENDY: And, like I said, I think his sister does, and we would've been the most important people to him. And, he had good friends, whom he liked, and they were very supportive of him.

MICHAEL: I just have this image of a young man who struggled with so much over such a period of his life. And that he persevered even with obligations to others. Like you mentioned the obligations he felt about the publication for children with cancer—that he met that obligation as best he could. Do you know what I mean? I'm just thinking about the context of his life, and, my guess is that he was pretty battle-weary toward the end.

WENDY: I think he really tried the last year.

MICHAEL: Yeah.

WENDY: More for us maybe even than for himself.

MICHAEL: So trying for the last year was out of his sense of loyalty and obligation, a sense of obligation?

WENDY: I think so. And I guess it's helping me see that he has let go of all that pain now.

MICHAEL: Yeah.

WENDY: So I don't have to carry it.

MICHAEL: Yeah.

WENDY: If it's gone for him. I mean the pain of his earlier years, if all that's gone, or if his misery is gone, then I shouldn't have to carry this on. Maybe it's then like a delay, trying to still look after him and care for him by carrying all this pain, but it's pretty pointless, really. It's not going to do anything to help that.

MICHAEL: I really appreciate what you've just said. I'd like to write it down. Would you say it again? About that he decided to let go of all that pain. He made that decision . . .

WENDY: I guess I've been still carrying that burden of his pain.

MICHAEL: Right.

WENDY: And suffering, because of it. But he's let go of it now. He's no longer in pain, so maybe I don't have to carry it anymore either.

MICHAEL: Yeah. If he could be here and hear you say that, how would he respond? Would he affirm that conclusion from what you know of him?

WENDY: I think he would. I think he would say, "Yes, you don't"—that I don't have to carry it, and that it's not helping him to do that.

MICHAEL: Yeah, so he'd say, "Yes, Mum." What words would he use if he were here? He was bright, he . . .

WENDY: He was very bright. He would probably have said that I did my best, that his decisions didn't have anything to do with anything on my part. That it was just his fate, I guess, to have a life of misery, and he had just decided he didn't want that anymore. And I would guess for him there would have been a loss of the ongoing contact with me and his sister too. I mean, I don't know what his beliefs about what happened after you die were. He used to describe himself as a "just-in-case" churchgoer: Once in a while he would go to church, just in case that was true. But he didn't exactly believe it, so . . .

MICHAEL: Sounds like quite a character, quite a character, your Ted.

WENDY: Yes, he was.

MICHAEL: Yeah. So he'd say something like, "Mum, I did my best. You've got to understand that I've made my decision to let go of the pain, and that's why it doesn't make sense for you to carry it on. And my decision wasn't connected to you; in fact, it was a decision that I could only make when I disconnected a little. And, you know, I've decided to take this step." Is that the sort of thing that he'd say? Would he call you "Mum?"

WENDY: Yeah.

MICHAEL: He'd say "Mum"?

WENDY: Yeah, and he . . .

MICHAEL: "I did my best"?

WENDY: And in his note he'd said that I was a strong person and that I could carry on.

MICHAEL: He'd want you to sort of make this reconnection that you're making and perhaps re-embrace some of the really special aspects about your connection with him?

WENDY: Yeah, I think he would.

MICHAEL: Yeah.

WENDY: I'm sure he would. I think what's hard is when the relationship has been so caught up in trauma. To reflect back on it even . . .

MICHAEL: It's painful.

WENDY: Well, it's painful, but also because so much of it was highly emotionally charged.

MICHAEL: Yeah.

WENDY: I couldn't get a sense of it always.

MICHAEL: Yeah.

WENDY: When I was in the hospital with him, I would try to do what I could for him. I remember one time, we were waiting and they put the file in the room and we were reading the file—which of course you should never do. And it contained comments about how when I brought him in, that he was much fussier and less satisfied with the work that they did, and that he kept complaining that they had to adjust him more often than when his father brought him in. My interpretation of that, or preferred interpretation, was that he felt he could say to me, "It hurts" and "Go ask them if they could change it," and I would do all of those things.

MICHAEL: And that he could respect his own experience of it and not be disqualified or made invisible by those routine ways of going about things that take place in hospitals that make people's experiences invisible.

WENDY: But it did make me doubt myself for a while. I thought maybe it's the sort of typical "mother-blaming" that often goes on. And maybe I was a difficult person for them to deal with in the sense that I would always try to be fairly polite and positive, but it was my belief that he could tell me when things hurt. And even if it would hurt just a little bit, why shouldn't it be adjusted for him?

MICHAEL: Yeah, exactly. But what was the hospital's interpretation of it?

WENDY: I think it was that I was a difficult mother. It was dishonoring me, dishonoring Ted, dishonoring his discomfort, and dishonoring the relationship between us, I felt.

MICHAEL: And disqualifying of *his* voice on it—it was just to do with you, not to do with his own voice. Would you say it was disqualifying of his voice?

WENDY: Yeah.

MICHAEL: So there was some dishonoring of your connection with him?

WENDY: I think so.

MICHAEL: We have to stop soon. I just want to reflect back on how this conversation has been going for you. What's been happening for you in the course of this conversation?

WENDY: It's been very helpful because it's put a different perspective on it, and I do feel a bit more freedom to remember whatever I want to remember, I suppose. Freedom from an obligation just to concentrate on the pain in his world. I feel that I can do that without disqualifying his pain. It was awful, but I don't have to keep carrying it anymore. And then I can think of some of the good moments in his life as well. I can think of some of those things. His energy and sense of humor and things like that. No, that's been very helpful. I appreciate that.

MICHAEL: Well, what thoughts do you have about steps that might follow this conversation? You've said some really powerful things, such as: "Ted did make a decision to let go of the pain, and it doesn't make sense that I should carry it on. And that he wouldn't want me to, and he would say, 'I did my best.'" And perhaps he would say: "You know, we got further down the track than maybe anyone could've expected under the circumstances, and that's a testimony to something that I don't want you to get disconnected from. This is not to say that I don't understand that you're also going through the pain of my death." And I'm just wondering what steps could follow from this for you?

WENDY: Well, I think I will be more freed up to remember enjoyable times, and his sister Caitlin will be a very willing participant in that, I'm sure. She'd be very supportive of that. And everyone's life is so complex and has so many experiences in it that I suppose you can be selective in what you look at. And I think he would prefer to be remembered for all his courage and for his brightness and his beauty and his sense of humor.

MICHAEL: And his perseverance, and . . .

WENDY: I remember Caitlin said once, "What if Ted's not going to be here?," talking about some particular occasion.

"Well, it won't be much fun without Ted." Because he very much "lived his life to the full"—in both good and bad experiences. But he certainly directed every situation he was in and organized it and energized it. So, that's a pretty good epitaph, I suppose, isn't it?

MICHAEL: Well, I wish I could've met your Ted, but in a way I have here today, 'cause you've been evoking his image here, and I'm very sad that Ted has struggled with what he's struggled with, but I guess, I'm also just aware of lots of other things too, you know, about what the fact of his existence stood for. So, I appreciate your speaking so freely about him and evoking his image here in the way that you have, even though you were very apprehensive about doing that in the first place. And if you'd like to have another conversation, I'd be happy to meet with you again.

WENDY: Oh, thanks Michael, I appreciate that. I'll see how I go, 'cause it might be helpful to follow up, and that's why I felt, if I taped it, then I could also revisit it.

MICHAEL: And if we don't catch up in the near future, you might drop me a line? Let me know where things have gone to since this conversation.

WENDY: Yeah, I think it should open up a different path, I hope. I feel as though a burden of his pain has been lifted.

MICHAEL: You feel that physically? Where do you feel that?

WENDY: Off my shoulders.

MICHAEL: Off your shoulders?

WENDY: Yeah. I feel less weighed down by this immense pain. So that's fantastic.

MICHAEL: That's quite something.

WENDY: Yeah, yeah it is. And I do feel more of a sense of reconnection with him. The sort of positive side of him, you know.

MICHAEL: Yeah.

WENDY: Because in many ways I think he was protective. He tried to be protective of me, to keep me from some of the awfulness, so that's good.

MICHAEL: What's that an act of?

WENDY: Pardon?

MICHAEL: What's that an act of?

WENDY: Yeah, an act of love.

MICHAEL: An act of love.

WENDY: Yeah.

I have not had the opportunity to study the cultural history of suicide or to study suicide as a phenomenon. But I do know that all forms of suicide in all cultures do not represent the ultimate transgression—in fact, in some circumstances, it has been considered to be an act of honor, in others an act of necessity. In our conversations with the friends, family, neighbors, and acquaintances of those who take their lives, it is possible to investigate and honor the "insider meanings" of suicide. Suicide comes to be seen as a mindful act, and in the process the person's life, and values, become visible again. Significantly, this can make it more possible for loved ones to feel linked with the person who has died.

CHAPTER 11

Couples Therapy

ENTERING COUPLES INTO AN ADVENTURE

We live in a culture that has a tradition of objectifying persons and relationships with problem descriptions; problems are considered to be inherent to persons or intrinsic to relationships. That is, persons and relationships are seen as the sources of the problems that persons experience in living. The problem is the person's character, or a personal deficit, or a personal shortcoming, or some quality of the relationship. In the psychologies, these practices are institutionalized through instruments for the classification of disorders within persons. One of these instruments, the DSM- III, has recently been spectacularly successful.

POSITIVISM

How did all of this "progress" come about? There are many developments, mostly interrelated, that contributed to the possibilities for the individualizing of persons and for the creation of internalizing discourses. One of the developments that has contributed to this individualization of persons is the rise of positivism. Positivism is an approach to the understanding of events in the world that proposes that it is possible to directly know the world—that it is possible for observers of certain phenomena to gain an objective knowledge of reality, to identify "brute facts," and to uncover the "truth" of the world. Positivism, in its attempts to come up with these truths, employs a reductionist method: It consistently endeavors to reduce the complexity of phenomena to basic elements, which are then considered to be the building blocks of the phenomena in question. These elements can be categorized and classified, and universal laws governing such phenomena in all places and at all times can be "discovered."

When positivism was applied to the human sciences, persons were subjected to the assessment of observers, armed with the techniques of evaluation, who were considered to be objective and thus not implicated in the construction of the realities being brought forth. Complex phenomena, as reflected in human behavior, were reduced to certain elements that were considered to be the building blocks of that behavior—such as certain traits, drives, needs, complexes of desire, etc. Behavior and social organization, considered to be in some way problematic, were assessed to be disorders in these basic elements, disorders that could be categorized and then classified. In this way, classification could represent the truth of the person.

In the history of the psychologies, we have seen the development of several major approaches to the understanding of human behavior and social organization that are informed by positivist thought. The most successful of these psychologies have been those that are premised upon the idea that human behavior and social organization reflect, in various ways, the structure of the mind or the emotional system. These are often referred to as the depth psychologies; their methods are informed by positivism, and they engage persons in internalizing discourses. Not only are these psychologies dominant in professional domains, but they have also been spectacularly successful in the domain of popular culture.

POST-POSITIVISM AND DECONSTRUCTION

In these notes, as an alternative to positivist therapy, I discuss practices of deconstruction particularly as they relate to work with couples. The externalization of the problem usually gives us a point of entry into these processes. Through a process of questioning, the externalization of phenomena becomes multilayered, tying further back into context as it is pursued. Thus, it tends to enter couples into an adventure.

Influence of the problem questions

INTERPRETATION QUESTIONS

These include those questions that relate to the conclusions, attitudes, and perceptions of the couple's relationship that seem to be inspired by the partners' experience of the problem. These questions introduce externalizing discourses. First, the problem is objectified, and then the conclusions are objectified:

- How do you see this problem reflecting on your relationship?
- Tell me about the conclusions, regarding your relationship, that this problem has led to.
- How has this problem affected your perception of your relationship?
- What sorts of opinions have you formed about your relationship since it has been under the influence of this problem?
- What sorts of observations about your relationship seem to be reinforced by this problem?

PRACTICES QUESTIONS

These include questions that relate to the practices, strategies, and techniques that appear to be dictated by the problem:

- In what ways do you think this problem has influenced your interaction with each other?
- In response to this problem, what strategies are you witnessing each other engage in?
- What techniques for dealing with each other do you feel compelled to resort to?

Real Effects Questions
EFFECTS OF INTERPRETATION QUESTIONS

These questions encourage persons to identify the real effects of these interpretations in terms of the responses of the partners and in terms of relationship practices:

- How do you think these conclusions have affected what you do in this relationship?
- How has this perception of your relationship influenced your responses to each other?
- In what way do you think these opinions may be shaping the patterns in your relationship?
- In what way do you think that these observations might have you second-guessing each other?

EFFECTS OF PRACTICES QUESTIONS

- What do you think these patterns are doing to your relationships?
- How are these strategies affecting your relationship?
- In what ways are these techniques shaping your relationship?

Context of Interpretation and Practices Questions
HISTORICAL DOMAIN

These questions encourage persons to identify the history of the experiences, knowledges, and practices that make the interpretations possible. These questions challenge those explanations based on the idea of volition, "interests," and destiny.

HISTORY OF EXPERIENCES

- What experiences have you had in the past that enabled you to reach these conclusions about your relationship?
- What events have contributed most in facilitating this perception of your relationship?
- What circumstances have you lived through that have assisted you most in forming this opinion about your relationship?
- Were these observations about your relationship arrived at easily? What experiences are they based upon?

HISTORY OF KNOWLEDGES

- What sort of view would you need to have of relationships in order to reach these conclusions?
- Historically, where did you get the view of relationships that provides the basis for this perception of your relationship? What is this view?
- What sort of expectations or specifications would you need to have for successful relationships in order to form this opinion about yours?
- Which ideas about relationships would you need to measure yours against in order to make these judgments?
- Is this a relationship, a friendship, an acquaintanceship, an economic or moral arrangement, a convenience, or something like an arch-rivalryship? Where does the model for this relationship come from?

HISTORY OF PRACTICES

- I usually find that most couples don't invent as much as they think they have. Where have you witnessed these practices before?

- Are these strategies unique to your relationship, or have you observed them in other relationships?
- Who first introduced you to, or what situation first exposed you to, these techniques of relationship?

DOMAIN OF SOCIAL SPACES/STRUCTURES

These questions encourage persons to identify the social spaces/structures that make the interpretations and practices possible.

- In what situations would you most expect to see those opinions about relationships circulating?
- What contexts are most likely to reinforce these ideas about how relationships should be?
- Who else is most likely to hold these views about relationships, and what is their position of influence?
- If you were to challenge these attitudes about relationships, from where would you experience most pressure to conform?
- What would be the cost to you socially if you decided to free your relationships from these practices? Whose expectations would you be most likely to upset?
- In what contexts would you expect to find these strategies most commonplace? What justifications are referred to in order to sustain them?
- In what locations are peoples' interactions determined by these techniques?

Recruitment Questions

These questions relate to the processes by which persons are recruited into specific knowledges and practices of relationship:

- How were you recruited into this view of how relationships should be?
- How did you get coached into shaping your relationship according to this prescription?
- What forces managed to press you into conforming to this version of relationships?
- How were you encouraged to live out your relationship through these practices?
- How was your support for these relationship tactics enlisted?

Effects of Recruitment Questions

- Being successfully recruited into this view, how has this shaped the course of your relationship?
- How has this recruitment affected your attitude toward your relationship? How has it had you treating your relationship?
- As recruits, in what ways do you think these practices are dictating the future of your relationship?

RECONSTRUCTION

These notes detail some of the deconstructive aspects of this approach, not the reconstructive aspects. Therefore, they are incomplete. Just as the process of deconstruction seeks to enter couples into an adventure, the process of reconstruction seeks to make it possible for people to become dramatically engaged with their own lives. Where possible, therapists and others can orient themselves to the mystery in all of this.

Reconstructive practices include unique outcome questions, reauthoring questions (including landscape-of-action ques-

tions and landscape-of-consciousness questions), transforma-
tion questions, alternative practices questions, circulation of
alternative knowledge questions, and so on. Also, in practice,
the work discussed here would always be framed by some analysis of gender issues and politics.

Epilogue: Continuing Conversations

Cheryl White

Bringing together this book of Michael's unpublished writings and considering the continuing legacies of his work involves looking to the past and to the future. It involves both personal and collective considerations. Michael and I knew each other for 37 years and lived together for the first 36 of these. Here I offer some of my own reflections and also include the perspectives of practitioners from many different countries. What makes this possible is the generosity of all those who responded to the following invitation:

> *G'day, this is Cheryl writing to you with a special request.*
>
> *You probably know that we're putting together a book of Michael White's unpublished writings. In going through these papers, we have come across some real gems. It's been a good process. While it's a tender task, it's also one that's been engaging and inspiring. The book is coming together really well, and it's nearly finished.*
>
> *After quite some thought, it was decided that we would invite practitioners from many different countries and cultures to be involved in developing the postscript. And that's why I'm writing to you now. I am wondering if you would like to contribute to it in some way.*
>
> *Within this postscript, we wish to consider the ways in which Michael's ideas are being carried on and engaged with in many different contexts. We've put together a series of questions and are now inviting a wide range of people to respond to these. People's responses will then be collated*

into a collective piece. We hope this will enable us to create a rich tapestry
of perspectives. Of course, we will acknowledge all those who contribute
to this process.

As soon as I sent out this invitation, we began to receive
thoughtful and heartfelt responses from many different parts
of the world. Before I convey what was included in these
responses, I first wish to take you back to a time before the
phrase *narrative therapy* had been coined. I want to paint for you
a picture of the social context that informed the development
of narrative practice. For it is only with an understanding of
this social context that the papers in this book, and the legacies
of Michael's work, can be fully appreciated.

Michael was born in 1948, just post-World War II. Here in
Australia, many of the men of our fathers' and grandfathers'
generations had served in the armed forces during both World
Wars. The generation of which we were a part grew up in the
shadow of these two wars, and then came the Vietnam War.
While we first met studying social work, Michael and I really got
to know each other through participating in an anti-Vietnam
war demonstration. These demonstrations represented a profound shift in the relationships between generations. We were
sure that the older generation had it wrong, that they quickly
reverted to military responses, and that they could not consider
alternatives. The older generation considered those of us who
were demonstrating to be idealistic, naïve, and that we were
being manipulated by hidden Communist forces. Their reactions didn't deter us. It was as if some of the younger generation
had risen up. When Australian troops were eventually brought
home, when it became obvious to most people that the protest
movement had been influential in contributing to changing
attitudes to the war, it was as if the social fabric of Australia
had changed in some way. It was as if we, the younger generation, now had a renewed confidence to question and challenge

authority. We no longer had an unquestioning agreement with the generations before us. It's not that we were rude or impolite, but we were empowered. We were energized. It was a time of possibilities. We thought the world was going to change, and that we were going to be a part of changing it.

This was also the era of Women's Liberation, which was later known as the feminist movement. Around us we saw families and relationships changing. Interactions between men and women, which had been taken for granted for so long, were shifting. Change felt possible, even inevitable, from many different directions.

Why is this social context relevant to mention here in considering Michael's work and the development of narrative practice? In my mind, it is directly relevant. We were of the times when social movements were challenging taken-for-granted authority in a range of areas. Initially, the focus was the Vietnam War and feminism. And then the focus changed. Along with many others, Michael became determined to challenge and put forward alternatives to the taken-for-granted authorities within mental health services and psychiatry.

From the 1960s onwards, writers such as Michel Foucault, Erving Goffman, R. D. Laing, Thomas Szasz, and Franco Basaglia began to critique routinely accepted practices within psychiatry and the influence of psychiatric understandings within society more generally. Consumer/survivor movements of those who had endured degradations within mental health institutions also began campaigning for change. We had seen a social movement stop a war, and another change the ways in which women and men relate to each other and to life. As people in many different countries became determined to alter the ways in which their societies responded to those in social and emotional distress, this became a passion in Michael's life. And it is this commitment that led to the development of what is now known as narrative therapy.

Alongside the optimism and determination that accompanied this commitment, there was also excitement, adventure, and collaboration. When Michael met David Epston in the early 1980s, their partnership was characterized by fun and enthusiasm. It was never a chore to stay up to the early hours talking about what others might call "work." Money was very scarce in our household in those days and long-distance calls were expensive. We would have to save up in order for Michael to call David in New Zealand. The conversations would go something like this: "You won't believe whom I saw today in therapy! There was a child who was doing this and there was this parent who was doing that and what I did was, and what I tried was, what didn't work is . . ." or, alternatively, "Eppy, I've just got to talk to you. I tried this and nothing worked and I've got to see them again tomorrow and I don't know what to do and how am I going to manage this?" This was a collaboration, a friendship, a mateship. It meant there was always a person whom Michael could ring up and with whom he could share all his raw mistakes and all of his hopes. The papers included in this book would not have existed without this.

There is another theme that I would like to mention about the past, before turning to consider the future. It relates to irreverence. The development of narrative ideas was a part of a determined and committed challenge to existing ideas in the mental health system. At the same time, there was irreverence and much laughter. Michael was somewhat zany, and I think this had something to do with our social backgrounds.

I grew up on a farm and my brother, Peter, was the first person in our family ever to finish high school. Michael came from a working-class family, and his sister was the first person in his family to finish high school. Social work and the mental health field was a fairly middle-class occupation when we entered it, and we didn't really relate in the usual ways. We were bold, we were raucous. I would say that we were even a bit crass at times. And there was a lot of laughter.

The fact that we were outsiders to the middle-class professions meant that Michael would often flip things around. When he was a consultant within psychiatric hospitals, it was commonly thought that people who were hearing voices, people who were experiencing psychosis, had nothing to offer. They were not seen as people who could speak to their own experience. They were not seen as people of integrity. Instead, they were seen as "the other," to be hidden away. When Michael was working at a state psychiatric hospital, the ways he related to people were different from the usual "professional" ways. There is a particular story that illustrates this.

In order to get to the psychiatric hospital, Michael used to walk from home across a park. One day, while walking, he lost the button on his pants and they came undone. It became a real problem to hold them up as he was walking. He eventually made it to the psychiatric hospital, however, and sat down to meet with Sam, who was a "patient" in the locked ward because he'd been hearing voices. The family therapy team was sitting behind the one-way screen. The conversation they shared went something like this:

MICHAEL: Sam, do you ever have fears about something happening that you don't want to have happen?

SAM: Of course.

MICHAEL: And do you ever have nightmares about things you are afraid of?

SAM: Yeah, sometimes I do.

MICHAEL: And have you ever had that situation where the nightmare then actually happens? It comes true? The thing you are really worried about actually happens?

SAM: Yes, sure. I know what you mean. That's happened to me quite a few times.

MICHAEL: Well, have you ever had that nightmare about your pants falling down around your ankles?

SAM: Yes I have!

MICHAEL: Well that happened to me coming here. I lost my button and my pants started falling down.

SAM: [*At this point, Sam became quite concerned.*] Oh, I know what that's like, to have this worst dread that could ever happen to you, and you think it's going to happen . . . and then it does. What did you do?

MICHAEL: Well it was bad, and I still haven't got a button. I'm sort of covering it up now. What do you think I should do?

SAM: You know what? I'll go back to the ward because I've got a pin for you.

Sam then returned with a pin and the consultation continued, building on the momentum and camaraderie that had been created. Meanwhile, the team behind the screen was enchanted because this interaction had flipped the usual power relations. The person who was living with voices was suddenly making a contribution to the therapist and literally helping him to keep his pants up. To Michael, this was a normal, dignifying, and *re-grading* conversation. But it was completely counter to the professional culture of the time. Inviting and acknowledging the suggestions, ideas, and contributions of "patients" was profoundly irregular at that time.

There is just one other theme from the past that I wish to mention before turning to the future. This relates to Michael's independent scholarly approach to originating therapeutic practices. Michael was not a conventional scholar. In fact, he was profoundly skeptical of conventional academia and research and remained outside of formal institutions throughout his working life. From the early 1980s onwards, he was determined to build an independent center that could foster creative thinking outside any bureaucracy. For most of his life, Michael's ideas were seen as outside the mainstream, even "radical." It has only been in recent years that narrative ideas have become accepted within many mainstream institutions. On the one hand, this move represents the continuation of Michael's commitment to challenge conventional understandings within the mental health system. On the other hand, it seems important to continue the independent scholarly development of narrative practices. Michael drew on two separate sources for ideas. Firstly, he drew on his extensive practice. He always spoke of how the development of narrative therapy was the result of co-research with the families with whom he consulted. Secondly, he drew on writers from outside the field (e.g., Bateson, Bruner, Myerhoff, Vygotsky, Foucault, Derrida, and Deleuze). He was introduced to many of these authors by David Epston. When Michael engaged with these writers, he did not just read them once or twice. He studied their writings. He read everything he could find that they had written, and many commentaries about their work. This is what I refer to as his scholarly approach.

I believe that this book, this collection of Michael's writings, conveys the themes that I have mentioned here:

- His passion and commitment to contribute to changing the power relations of the mental health system
- The excitement, enthusiasm, and collaborative sense of adventure that characterized Michael's and David's constant invention of new ideas and practices
- The irreverence and humor that infused Michael's relationships with those with whom he worked
- An independent scholarly approach that rigorously combined practice with the development of new ideas.

There is just one more point. Michael was a hard worker. Throughout his working life, Michael saw families, wrote and taught with a vigor and determination that meant that he came in contact with practitioners from a very wide range of cultures and countries. As a result, his ideas have taken root in an extraordinary diversity of contexts. Thanks to the responses of some of these practitioners, I will now outline some of the ripples of Michael's work and how therapists and community workers in many different countries are continuing to originate narrative ways of working.

NARRATIVE RESPONSES TO TRAUMA: FROM RWANDA TO PALESTINE

Some of the most significant continuing developments in relation to narrative practice relate to responses to trauma. Counselors from Ibuka, the national genocide survivors' association in Rwanda, in partnership with Dulwich Centre Foundation International, are at the forefront of developing ways in which narrative therapy ideas can be used to work with problems of memory caused by significant trauma (see Denborough, 2010a; Denborough, Freedman, & White, 2008). Palestinian therapists at the Treatment and Rehabilitation Center in Ramallah are similarly developing forms of narrative practice that are culturally resonant (see Abu-Rayyan, 2009).

ORGANIZATIONAL CONSULTANCY AND COACHING

In Europe and elsewhere, the ideas of narrative practice are now being used within organizational consultancy, coaching, and work communities. This is particularly true in Denmark and France (see Blanc-Sahnoun, 2010; Freedman & Combs, 2009; Laplante & De Beer*; Sørensen*). Here Pierre Blanc-Sahnoun explains:

We are using narrative approaches to respond to work-communities confronted with suicide in the workplace; hardship and
economic crisis; redundancy plans; the destruction of local
plants; and so on. In our work, we work with local management
to bring to light that "resistance to change" is not a dysfunc-
tion but a proof of collective intelligence and a tribute to local
hopes and values. We find ways to deconstruct the global story
of "managerial performance" in the hope of building powerful and harmonious work-communities and respectful work-
cultures and practices. (Blanc-Sahnoun*)

CONTINUING THEORETICAL EXPLORATIONS

Following the lead of David Epston and Michael White, a number
of narrative practitioners are continuing to engage with and draw
inspiration from ideas outside the field of therapy. This includes
engaging with the writings of Deleuze (Carey*; Winslade, 2009),
Vygotsky (Kutuzova*), Ricoeur, Revel, Levi, and Proust (Laplante
& De Beer*). And David Epston continues to introduce new writers and thinkers to the field (including Hilde Lindemann Nelson).
One of Michael's concepts that practitioners continue to explore
involves the "absent but implicit." We believe that Chapter 9 of
this book, "Revaluation and Resonance: Narrative Responses to
Traumatic Experience," will provide practitioners with additional
thinking tools in relation to this concept. For other recent writings
on this topic, see Carey, Walther, and Russell (2009) and *Working
with Memory in the Shadow of Genocide: The Work of the Trauma Counselors of Ibuka* (Denborough, 2010a).

RESEARCH

While Michael was skeptical of what he termed *secondary
research* (along with David Epston, he understood therapy to

be a form of direct co-research with families), a wide range of creative research projects about narrative therapy are now underway. Many of these are documented in a recent research repository on the Dulwich Centre website (www.dulwichcentre.com.au/narrative-therapy-research.html). This repository includes information about Lynn Vromans' groundbreaking research on the process and outcome of narrative therapy (Vromans & Schweitzer, 2010), John Stillman's current research on narrative therapy and trauma (Stillman*); and Jim Duvall and Laura Béres's explorations connecting narrative therapy practice, training, and research (Duvall & Béres, in press).

NARRATIVE PRACTICE TO SPARK SOCIAL ACTION AND ECONOMIC DEVELOPMENT

The work of Caleb Wakhungu and the Mt. Elgon Self-Help Community Project, based in rural Uganda, is a vivid example of the ripples of Michael's teaching. Michael taught in Uganda in 2006, and narrative concepts are now being used in Mt. Elgon to spark a wide range of social action and economic development projects as well as to "raise people's heads above the clouds" (Wakhungu*). These projects involve children, young people, and adults and the results are inspiring. If there is one project we would wish Michael could witness, this would be the one (see Denborough, 2010b).

FOUND IN TRANSLATION

As therapists who work in languages other than English engage with narrative ideas, the process of translation is creating new forms of practice. This is a process that promises to bring new understandings and ways of working to the field. With this in mind, Marcela Polanco, Natasha Savelieva, and Daria Kutuzova have formed the "Found in Translation" project (see also Polanco & Epston, 2009; Uribe*; Grandesso*). These explorations are diverse. They range from Yishai Shalif's engagements with narrative ideas within Orthodox Jewish communities in Israel (Shalif*), to Sekneh Hammoud-Beckett's creative practice with young people of Muslim heritage in Sydney, Australia, which she describes here:

> I was born to a Lebanese Muslim family with a rich storytelling tradition. Throughout my childhood, I was surrounded by the folklore of the *Tales of the Arabian Nights*. When working with other Arabic speakers, narrative practices connect me to ways of telling stories that preserve and honor our lives. There are, however, complexities. For example, within the Arabic language, nouns are either referred to as masculine or feminine. Underlying expectations and meanings in relation to gender are implicit within the very words we speak. The narrative perspective supports me to respond to the dilemmas this sometimes evokes. It invites me to take a position of curiosity and respect in addressing the ways in which history, politics, and context shape our lives, and to loiter around the effects of forms of language, rather than impose universal Western understandings. (Hammoud-Beckett*).

DIVERSE FORMS OF THERAPEUTIC DOCUMENTATION

The book that ushered in the development of narrative therapy was entitled *Narrative Means to Therapeutic Ends* (White & Epston, 1990) and introduced the notion of therapeutic letters and documentation to the therapy field. Narrative therapists are now continuing to explore the use of diverse forms of documentation, including living documents that are developed over time and contributed to by different people (Newman, 2008);

cartoons (Ord & Emma, 2009); drawings (Colic, 2007); songs (Denborough, 2002, 2008; Wever, 2009; Hegarty, 2009); "narragrams" (Bera*); and talismans (Kutuzova*). Some practitioners are transforming routine reports to other professionals into collaboratively written documents of identity (Stockell*). Furthermore, collective narrative documents (Denborough, 2008) are now being engaged with in many different contexts, including Vietnam (Stillman*) and Mexico (Diaz-Smith*). A recent narrative project involving documentation was conducted by Carry Gorney in the United Kingdom, whereby she videorecorded sweet moments and interactions between young mothers and their babies. So successful was this project in supporting young "at-risk" mothers that it is now being replicated in refugee communities in Liverpool (Fox*). The possibilities for diverse forms of narrative therapeutic documentation seem limitless.

WORKING WITH ABORIGINAL COMMUNITIES

From the mid-1980s onwards, Michael worked in partnership with Aboriginal Australian colleagues, and the legacies of these partnerships continue. Barbara Wingard remains actively involved in the work of the Dulwich Centre Foundation in a range of different projects in Aboriginal communities. One of these projects recently culminated in the publication and recording *Yia Marra: Good Stories That Keep Spirits Strong—from the People of Ntaria/Hermannsburg* (Denborough, Wingard, & White, 2009). Aboriginal colleagues in different communities are also engaged with the Tree of Life narrative approach (Dulwich Centre Foundation, 2009). And Barbara Wingard has also recently developed an externalizing conversations script in relation to "lateral violence" (Wingard, 2010) in order to facilitate helpful dialogue about conflict within Aboriginal communities. In other developments, narrative approaches have been creatively embraced by Link-Up workers who respond to Aboriginal people who are trying to reconnect with family members from whom they have been separated. As Shona Russell describes, "these are ways in which narrative practices are being used in response to the ongoing effects of historical injustice in Australia" (Russell*).

Michael was also involved in the Neighbouring Communities project in 2006/2007 outside Toronto, Ontario. This project sought to address conflict between the people of the Six Nations Reserve and the citizens of Caledonia, which had resulted from a land claim dispute. Positive effects from this project continue (Duvall*).

RIGOROUS NARRATIVE THERAPY TRAINING PROGRAMS

There are now more opportunities than ever for practitioners to be trained in narrative approaches. Workshops and training programs are now available in a wide range of countries including Australia, New Zealand, Israel, and North America, and the options keep expanding. Recent developments include extended training programs in narrative therapy being established in Singapore and Greece. A new institute has been established in the United Kingdom, and further European narrative therapy conferences are planned. A 3-year program is also underway in partnership between Dulwich Centre and the Trauma and Rehabilitation Center for Victims of Torture and Trauma in Ramallah, Palestine. And this is in addition to the Dulwich Centre International Graduate Diploma in Narrative Therapy and Community Work, which continues to accept practitioners from different parts of the world every 2 years. Other developments in relation to narrative therapy training include Martha Campillo's (2009) book in Spanish on teaching narrative practices and Geir Lundby's development of the "stair of questions" in assisting people to engage with the scaffolding map of narrative practice (Lundby*). Over the last 5 years, through Tod Augusta-Scott's training, Michael's ideas have been presented in relation to working with men whose abuse has had a significant impact on the populations of four provinces that make up Atlantic Canada (Augusta-Scott*). But these are just a few of the developments in relation to training. It seems that every second week there is a new announcement in relation to training programs in narrative therapy in different parts of the world.

NARRATIVE PRACTICES OUTSIDE THE THERAPY DOMAIN

Increasingly, narrative ideas are being engaged not only within counseling and therapy rooms but also in a wide range of other domains: for example, within approaches to school bullying, as well as within mediation and restorative justice projects (Winslade*). The Tree of Life narrative approach (Ncube, 2006; see also www.dulwichcentre.com.au/tree-of-life.html) is now being widely used with children in schools and in group contexts, as is the Team of Life (Denborough, 2008), which draws upon sporting metaphors to enable young people to deal with traumatic experience without having to speak directly about it. The development of both these methodologies began during trips to Africa that Michael was a part of in the last years of his life. Another example is the "hero book" developed by Jonathan Morgan:

> Michael [White] and David Epston's work formed the basis of the hero book which is literally a physical "hard copy" re-authored life story document fashioned and crafted together with paper, string, and ink. In the African context, this work is at an exciting phase as hero books are now being mainstreamed into the national curricula and syllabi whereby pupils in the

classroom, during school time, make their own hero books over one or two terms in the academic year. Via this mainstreaming approach and in collaboration with governments, this has the potential to reach literally millions of children. I think Michael would have been interested to witness this development and to see his influence unfold in this way. I think he would have enjoyed seeing children with hero books written in Swahili, Zulu, Nepalese, Arabic, etc., especially the pages in which the children draw their wishes and goals, as well as the named externalized obstacles that stand in the way of these goals, and the pages entitled "Club of Life," "Tricks and Tactics," and "Re-Membering Party" (Morgan*).

Virtual Narrative Practices and the Creation of Communities

The realm of the Internet is increasingly significant in the distribution and further originating of narrative practices. Take, for instance, the work of Daria Kutuzova, who has made available a range of free-access online publications in Russian:

These have been found and explored by people from all walks of life. The narrative approach gives people in a society where the sense of community was destroyed tools to enhance the rebuilding of communities, starting first in the Internet though creation of communities united by shared concern, and gradually taking these project into "real life" ("offline") space. The narrative worldview with its respectful attitude to the interlocutor, with its accent on community and enabling contribution, linking lives around shared themes and exploring new territories of identity, is becoming a (sub)cultural phenomenon, inspiring people to create enclaves of alternative forms of communication with oneself and others, and providing tools for the realization of this. For example, the narrative practices of "witnessing" and "definitional ceremony" were taken up by organizers of the first "undercover" queer Christian conference in Russia (it had to be "undercover" for security reasons, because homophobia, ignorance, and aggression are quite strong in our society), and it made the atmosphere of this conference so much more open to celebration of diversity. (Kutuzova*)

Online training in narrative therapy is also increasing (see Sax, 2008; Sax & Hughes*), and Narrative Connections: An International Network of Narrative Practitioners (www.dulwichcentre.com.au/narrative-connections.html) now contains members from 37 countries. From members' listings can be found links to a wide range of websites and blogs relating to narrative practice in a range of different languages.

The launch in 2009 of *Explorations: An E-Journal of Narrative Practice* was another key development in the dispersal of narrative ideas and stories of practice. It is hoped that this free e-journal, which involves supporting organizations from many different parts of the world, will provide avenues for support of narrative practitioners in countries where there are few resources or training/supervision options currently available, such as Maksuda Begum, who is trying to introduce narrative approaches in Bangladesh (Begum, 2007).

Michael's Ideas as a Foundation to
Respond to Communities in Hardship

In the years since Michael's death, his ideas have been used to respond to a wide range of communities who are enduring hardship. The Dulwich Centre Foundation has been established for just this purpose. A recent project has just taken place in Srebrenica, Bosnia. For more information, see (www.facebook.com/pages/Dulwich-Centre-Foundation/30531674546). "Collective narrative practice" in response to groups and communities who are experiencing hardship is an emerging field of practice (Denborough, 2008).

NARRATIVE PRACTICES WITHIN MENTAL HEALTH

As Michael was so determined to influence the field of mental health practice, it seems important to include examples of narrative practice now occurring within psychiatric institutions. One example can be found in the University Clinic for Psychiatry for Children and Adolescents in Salzburg, Austria:

> Even though I have been working for a long time from a narrative perspective in my outpatient work, it has been only recently that we have been trying to implement narrative ideas and practices on the ward for children and adolescents. Our most recent project is the conceptualisation of a therapeutic group on our ward for adolescents. The working title of the group is "liberation from inner destructive voices." Michael White's ideas about externalizing conversations are very well established in the ongoing therapeutic work in our clinic. In this group for young people who struggle with hateful and destructive thoughts about themselves, we try to offer some help in distancing from these "inner voices" and discovering subordinate storylines in their lives and relationships. Among other things, we use letters that come from other young persons that are faced with similar problems. These letters involve questions to the group that are supposed to stimulate a critical examination and an exposé of these problems. In the clinical context I work in, I can imagine the development of a concept for the in-patient stay that is narratively influenced. (Kronbichler*)

A second key example is the work of Ruth Pluznick and Natasha Kis-sines in working with families in which a parent or caregiver has a serious mental health difficulty (Pluznick & Kis-sines, 2008, 2010). Not only is the work providing space for young people and adults to reclaim their relationships from the effects of mental health difficulties, it is also posing the question "what becomes possible when we give up on the idea of 'normal families'"? (Pluznick*).

There are many other examples of narrative therapy ideas now being engaged with in mental health settings, from day treatment programs in the United States (Kazan*) to mental health rehabilitation services in Australia (O'Neill*) to psych-oeducation in Japan (Komori*).

LIVES OF THERAPISTS: PERSONAL REFLECTIONS

Michael was vitally interested in how narrative practices influence the lives of therapists as well as the lives of those who consult therapists (see White, 1997). Having briefly surveyed the enormous diversity of ways in which narrative ideas are being carried forth and reinvigorated within the professional field, it seems appropriate to also include two reflections from therapists about continuing personal legacies. Of all Michael's writings, perhaps "Saying Hullo Again" (1988/1998) and his invitations to restore relationships with those who have passed away have been most commonly mentioned by therapists as influential in their own lives (Hedtke* ; Navartnam*). As Cuqui Toledo from México explains:

> I am going to answer this question in a different way, with my own experience. The first time Michael came to México, I met him and thanked him for the wonderful article "Saying Hullo Again." I told him it had really helped me to have the energy to keep going. When I was telling him how my son had died of AIDS, a few months before, I saw tears in his eyes. I

thought pollution in the city's air was the trouble, but when I asked him, he said: "My tears are because I can feel the pain you have been through with this experience." That was the moment when I decided I wanted to be this kind of therapist, to be able to join with people the way Michael had been with me. (Toledo*)

Kaethe Weingarten similarly describes:

Prior to today, I would have said that it was Michael's frameworks for bridging the macro world analysis of socio-political conditions with the micro-politics of every day life that most inspires my practice: both what I do and what I write. This day I see that at many critical moments in our family's life, narrative ideas have provided a foundation for meaning-making that has been constructive and enlivening, easing shame, doubt, and grief and encouraging curiosity and momentum. I think the future of Michael's work lies in just this kind of insight: the personal is the professional and vice versa. I have had many such "ah ha" moments and each has strengthened me in all of my roles. Local adaptations of narrative therapy will come from people who not just admire narrative ideas but from people whose lives have been changed by them. (Weingarten*)

One further personal anecdote seems significant to include, this time from Jeff Zimmerman:

I remember a conversation I had with Michael in the late 1980s. I had been doing work applying narrative therapy ideas to working with couples. As usual, Michael seemed genuinely curious about my ideas. After I shared my thinking, Michael said, "That seems like a really good way to do it." Aside from the immediate good effects on me of this comment, a door was opened . . .

freedom! There were many ways one could do the work we do. (Zimmerman*)

OUTSIDER-WITNESS PRACTICE AS A FRIEND

One of the places in which this freedom to engage with narrative therapy ideas is being vividly expressed is Hong Kong. As Angela Tsun on-Kee describes, Michael's ideas have become a "friend" to practitioners there. This is particularly true in relation to outsider-witness practices, which Michael would often refer to as the most powerful therapeutic practice with which he was familiar.

> We could never imagine the meaning of outsider-witness practices until we witnessed their impact not only on the persons with whom we were working, but also on our own personal and professional identities. Many social service agencies here in Hong Kong have been developing innovative projects using outsider-witness practice with persons from different walks of life: elderly people, young people, parents and groups that are marginalized. One of these projects, called the Life Bank, is using outsider-witness practice to connect and re-connect young people who have used drugs, young people who have not used drugs, parents with children who have taken drugs, and parents of children who have not taken drugs. But there are many other projects too, including those concerning experiences of sexual harassment/abuse, and young same-sex attracted people. Michael's ideas have become our friends. (Tsun on-Kee*)

THE FUTURE

As this epilogue draws to a close, and as we turn toward the future, it seems fitting to include the words of Brazilian therapists. The ways in which Brazilian practitioners are engaging with narrative ideas was of great interest to Michael. He marveled at the vibrancy and thoughtfulness of those he had spent time with in Brazil. The year 2011 will see the 10th International Narrative Therapy and Community Work Conference take place in Salvador, Brazil. No doubt, this event will provide impetus for the further development of diverse forms of narrative practice. One particularly exciting development involves how Marilene Grandesso is combining narrative therapy practices with what is known as "community therapy":

> One local innovation is the union of Community Therapy, created in Brazil by psychiatrist Adalberto Barreto, with narrative practices. At the institute that I coordinate, we have had the opportunity to work with communities as partners, not only in re-authoring their participants' individual stories, but also constructing a collective "tissue" that covers organising narratives of collective identities. In Community Therapy, the use of collective narrative documents in final rituals gives visibility and enables fragments of conversation to remain present, transforming them in an aesthetic patchwork. (Grandesso*)

Another Brazilian therapist, Maria Angela Teixeira, explains eloquently how practitioners are continuing to originate forms of narrative therapy:

> Just as writers create something new by using the words available to us all, so too I hope that as narrative practitioners here in Brazil we will create new forms of narrative therapy. We will use the words, concepts, and practices offered to us by the initiators, Michael White and David Epston, and create something new with them. This will be our way of showing gratitude and honor. (Teixeira*)

This spirit is congruent with the history of the development of narrative therapy that I outlined at the beginning of this chapter. Whereas narrative therapy first developed in Australia and New Zealand and using the English language, as this postscript describes, the future of narrative practice lies in the diversity of narrative practitioners. Some of the most exciting developments are now taking place in Africa, Asia, the Middle East, and South America, and the conversations are occurring in Spanish, Portuguese, Arabic, Chinese, Hebrew, and so on.

What is also significant is that people outside the professions are now engaging with and transforming narrative practices. As Angel Yuen describes:

> It has been encouraging and promising to see community people from diverse backgrounds starting to engage with narrative practices within their own communities. This has included community leaders, pastors, consumers of mental health services, and community workers from varied cultures. Hence it is exciting to imagine the futures of narrative practice with more platforms being created for children, youth, and adults from diverse and marginalized communities to share their voices, skills, and knowledges with others. My everlasting wish is that collectively we will find ways to utilize our power and privilege as professionals to open up possibilities for our vulnerable children and young people today to become some of the future voices and leaders of narrative practice in the field. (Yuen*)

This process is underway. It will require continuing efforts. Alongside all the other contributing factors, hard work and a collaborative sense of adventure were two key ingredients in the development of what is now known as narrative therapy. As we all work to continue the legacies of Michael's ideas, what is profoundly reassuring is just how many of us are involved in this project, and just how different we are from one another.

NOTE

*A wide range of practititioners sent in written contributions to this epilogue. An asterix next to an author's name indicates one of these contributions. To view an edited collection of these writings see: www.dulwichcentre.com.au/michael-white-archive.html

Postscript and Acknowledgment

Cheryl White

Abook about Michael's work would not be complete without an acknowledgment to Karl Tomm. We first met Karl in the mid-1980s when he was on a teaching tour of Australia. This meeting sparked the beginning of long-term and enduring friendships. Karl was pretty impressive. As well as being a skilled practitioner, he had a passionate interest in theory. Our discussions were intense as ideas flew between us. He was intrigued by Michael's work and on returning to Canada he actively "opened space" for Michael's voice and ideas to be shared in the northern hemisphere. Given that Michael was a young working-class social worker from Adelaide and that Karl was a senior professor of psychiatry from Canada, this was an extraordinary act of inclusivity. When Karl was invited to teach workshops, he said to the organizers that he would like to share the space with someone who was doing exciting work. I think the workshop organizers were quite surprised when they learned that Karl was referring to a young man of whom they'd never heard who lived in Australia!

Karl, however, was a highly respected clinician and teacher, and so people trusted his judgment and Karl and Michael began teaching together. Actually, it seems important to mention that Karl insisted on this. He told organizers he would *only* take up their invitations to teach if he could do so jointly with Michael. This really was an extraordinary act. It could be minimized as an act of personal generosity or the celebration of a friendship, but it was far more than this. This was an act of a senior person who used his privilege to introduce the ideas and work of someone else. To do this involved sharing the teaching fee, stepping back from center stage, and entering into a partnership with a younger presenter.

One of the first workshop organizers to accept Karl's proposal and to host a workshop taught jointly by Karl and Michael was Gail Lapidus, from Tulsa, Oklahoma. Gail said that, in the Jewish community of which she is a part, this act of Karl's made perfect sense. She said that Karl was acting as a "good Rabbi/ teacher." She explained that, in her tradition, "good Rabbis" find ways to open space for the ideas of the next wave of thinkers.

Karl Tomm was terrific. He was inspiring, supportive, and full of energy and fun. Without Karl's commitment, it is possible that Michael's work would not have been known outside of Australia and New Zealand. What Karl offered was an entrée into a world otherwise closed to someone like Michael. It was a world that was strange and at times frightening to us, but Karl's confidence eased the way.

When I consider the future of the narrative therapy field, I can't help but wonder what our field would look like if we continued Karl's tradition of "opening space" for those who are not currently a part of our mainstream professional culture, but who are bubbling over with excitement around ideas, innovating as they go, and are grappling with what good narrative practice would look like in their own cultural contexts. What would it mean if those voices were given a space on the stage? What would it mean if we learn from Karl and use our privilege, resources, and courage to bring forth the next wave of narrative practice?

References

Abu-Rayyan, N. M. (2009). Seasons of Life: Ex-detainees reclaiming their lives. *The International Journal of Narrative Practice and Community Work*, (2), 24–40.

Bachelard, G. (1994). Introduction. In G. Bachelard, *The poetics of space* (M. Jolas, Trans., pp. xv–xxxix). Boston, MA: Beacon. (Original work published 1958)

Bauman, Z. (2000). *Liquid modernity*. Cambridge, England: Polity Press.

Bauman, Z. (2001). Stories told and lives lived. In Z. Bauman, *The individualized society* (pp. 1–16). Cambridge, England: Polity Press.

Beck, U. (1992). *Risk society: Towards a new modernity*. London, England: Sage.

Begum, M. (2007). Conversations with children with disabilities and their mothers. *The International Journal of Narrative Practice and Community Work*, (3), 11–16.

Blanc-Sahnoun, P. (2009). Narrative coaching in a professional community after a suicide. *Explorations: An E-Journal of Narrative Practice*, (1), 17–25. Retrieved from www.dulwichcentre.com.au/explorations-2009–1-pierre-blanc-sahnoun.pdf

Campillo, M. R. (2009) *Terapia narrativa: Auto–aprendizaje y co-aprendizaje grupal*. Xalapa, México: Publicaciones Ollin-Marta Campillo.

Caputo, J. (1993). On not knowing who we are: Madness, hermeneutics and the night of truth. In J. Caputo & M. Yount (Eds.), *Foucault and the critique of institutions*. University Park, PA: Penn State University Press.

Carey, M., Walther, S., & Russell, S. (2009). The absent but implicit: A map to support therapeutic enquiry. *Family Process, 48*(3), 319–331. doi:10.1111/j.1545–5300.2009.01285.x

Colic, M. (2007). Kanna's lucid dreams and the use of narrative practices to explore their meaning. *The International Journal of Narrative Therapy and Community Work*, (4), 19–26.

Cowley, G., & Springen, K. (1995). Rewriting life stories. *Newsweek*, April 17, 70–74.

Denborough, D. (2002). Community song writing and narrative practice. *Clinical Psychology*, 17, 17–24.

Denborough, D. (2008). *Collective narrative practice: Responding to individuals, groups, and communities who have experienced trauma.* Adelaide, Australia: Dulwich Centre Publications.

Denborough, D. (2010a). *Working with memory in the shadow of genocide: The narrative practices of Ibuka trauma counsellors.* Adelaide, Australia: Dulwich Centre Foundation International.

Denborough, D. (Ed.) (2010b) *Raising our heads above the clouds: The use of narrative practices to motivate social action and economic development: The work of Caleb Wakhungu and the Mt Elgon Self-Help Community Project.* Adelaide, Australia: Dulwich Centre Foundation International.

Denborough, D., Freedman, J., & White, C. (2008). *Strengthening resistance: The use of narrative practices in working with genocide survivors.* Adelaide, Australia: Dulwich Centre Foundation.

Denborough, D., Wingard, B., & White, C. (2009). *Yia Marra: Good stories that make spirits strong—from the people of Ntaria/Hermannsburg.* Adelaide & Alice Springs, Australia: Dulwich Centre Foundation & General Practice Network NT.

Denzin, N. (2003). *Performance ethnography: Critical pedagogy and the politics of culture.* Thousand Oaks, CA: Sage Publications.

Didion, J. (2003). *The year of magical thinking.* New York, NY: Vintage.

Dreyfus, J. L., & Rabinow, P. (1983). *Michel Foucault: Beyond structuralism and hermeneutics* (2nd ed.). Chicago, IL: University of Chicago Press.

Dulwich Centre Foundation (2009). *Finding hidden stories of strength and skills: Using the Tree of Life with Aboriginal and Torres Strait Islander children* [DVD]. Adelaide, Australia: Dulwich Centre Foundation.

Duvall, J. & Béres, L. (in press) *Innovations in narrative therapy: Connecting practice, training, and research.* New York, NY: W. W. Norton.

Duvall, J., & Young, K. (2009). Keeping faith: A conversation with Michael White. *Journal of Systemic Therapies, 28*(1), 1–18. doi:10.1521/jsyt.2009.28.1.1.

Epston, D. (1998). Voices. In D. Epston, *'Catching up' with David Epston: A collection of narrative practice-based papers published between 1991 & 1996* (pp. 33–38). Adelaide, Australia; Dulwich Centre Publications. New York, NY: W. W. Norton. Reprinted from *Strange encounters with Carl Auer*, by G. Weber & F. B. Simon, (Eds.) 1991.

Epston, D. (2010). What I would be doing if I were with you! [Address to the Narrative Therapy as Contextual Practice in South Africa Conference, Cape Town, October 12/13, 2009]. *Explorations: An E-Journal of Narrative Practice*, (1), 92–94. Retrieved from www.dulwichcentre.com.au/explorations-2010–1-david-epston.pdf

Epston, D., & White, M. (1985). *Consulting your consultant's consultants*. Workshop notes, Fifth Australian Family Therapy Conference, Sydney, Australia.

Epston, D., & White, M. (1992). *Experience, contradiction, narrative and imagination: Selected papers of David Epston and Michael White, 1989–1991*. Adelaide, Australia: Dulwich Centre Publications.

Epston, D., White, M., & Murray, K. (1998). A proposal for a re-authoring therapy: Rose's revisioning of her life and a commentary. In D. Epston, *"Catching up" with David Epston: A collection of narrative practice-based papers published between 1991 & 1996* (pp. 9–32). Adelaide, Australia; Dulwich Centre Publications. Reprinted from *Therapy as social construction*, by S. McNamee & K. Gergen, Eds., 1992, London, England: Sage Publications.

Faris, W. B. (2004). *Ordinary enchantments: Magical realism and the remystification of narrative*. Nashville, TN: Vanderbilt University Press.

Foucault, M. (1982). Truth, power, self: An Interview with Michel Foucault (25 October 1982). In Martin, L. H., Gutman, H., & Hutton, P., (Eds.) 1988. *Technologies of the self: A seminar with Michel Foucault* (pp. 9–15). London, England: Tavistock.

Fraenkel, P. (2005). Whatever happened to family therapy? *Psychotherapy Networker, 29*, 30–39, 70.

Freedman, J., & Combs, G. (2009). Narrative ideas for consulting with communities and organizations: Ripples from the gatherings. *Family Process 48*(3), 347–362. doi:10.1111/j.1545-5300.2009.01287.x

Galeano, E. (1992). *The book of embraces.* New York, NY: W. W. Norton.

Galeano, E. (2006). *Ceremony in voices of time: A life in stories.* New York, NY: Picador.

Geertz, C. (1983). *Local knowledge: Further essays in interpretive anthropology.* New York, NY: Basic Books.

Giddens, A. (1992). *Modernity and self-identity: Self and society in the late modern age.* Palo Alto, CA: Stanford University Press.

Hall, R. (1994). Partnership accountability. *Dulwich Centre Newsletter,* (2&3), 6–29.

Hegarty, T. (2009). Songs as re-tellings. *The International Journal of Narrative Therapy and Community Work,* (3), 44–54.

Hejinian, L. (2000). *The language of inquiry.* Berkeley, CA: University of California Press.

James, W. (1890). *The principles of psychology* (Vol. 1, trs. 1918). New York, NY: Dover.

Judt, T. (2010a, April 29–May 12). Ill fares the land. *New York Review of Books.*

Judt, T. (2010b). *Ill fares the land.* New York, NY: Penguin.

King, J., & Epston, D. (2009). Unsuffering myself and my daughter from anorexia. Manuscript submitted for publication.

Lindemann Nelson, H. (2001). *Damaged identities, narrative repair.* Ithaca, NY: Cornell University Press.

Madigan, S. (in press). *Who has the story-telling rights to the story being told?: Narrative therapy theory and practice.* Washington, DC: American Psychological Association.

Maisel, R., Epston, D., & Borden, A. (2004). *Biting the hand that starves you: Inspiring resistance to anorexia/bulimia.* New York, NY: W. W. Norton.

Mauss, M. (1954). *The gift: Forms and functions of exchange in archaic societies* (I. Cunnison, Trans.). London, England: Cohen and West.

McLeod, J. (2004). The significance of narrative and storytelling in postpsychological counseling and psychotherapy. In A. Lieblich, D. McAdams, & R. Josselson (Eds.), *Healing plots: The narrative basis for psychotherapy* (pp. 11–27). Washington, DC: American Psychological Association.

McLeod, J. (2005). Counseling and psychotherapy as cultural work. In L. T. Hoshmand (Ed.), *Culture, psychotherapy and counseling: cri-*

tical and integrative perspectives (pp. 47–64). Thousand Oaks, CA: Sage.

McLeod, J. (2006). Narrative thinking and the emergence of post-psychological therapies. *Narrative Inquiry, 16*(1), 201–210. doi:10.1075/ni.16.1.25mcl

Murray, K. (1985). Life as fiction. *Journal for the Theory of Social Behaviour, 15*, 173–187. doi: 10.1111/j.1468-5914.1985.tb00050.x

Myerhoff, B. (1980). *Number our days.* New York, NY: Simon & Schuster.

Myerhoff, B. (1982). Life history among the elderly: Performance, visibility, and re-membering. In J. Ruby (Ed.), *A crack in the mirror: Reflexive perspectives in anthropology* (pp. 99–117). Philadelphia, PA: University of Pennsylvania Press.

Myerhoff, B. (1986). Life not death in Venice: Its second life. In Turner, V. & Bruner, E. (Eds.), *The anthropology of experience* (pp. 261–286). Chicago, IL: University of Illinois Press.

Ncube, N. (2006). The Tree of Life Project: Using narrative ideas in work with vulnerable children in Southern Africa. *The International Journal of Narrative Therapy and Community Work*, (1), 3–16.

Newman, D. (2008). "Rescuing the said from the saying of it": Living documentation in narrative therapy. *The International Journal of Narrative Therapy and Community Work*, (3), 24–34.

Ord, P., & Emma. (2009). The therapeutic use of a cartoon as a way to gain influence over a problem. *The International Journal of Narrative Therapy and Community Work*, (1), 14–17.

Pluznick, R., & Kis-Sines, N. (2008). Growing up with parents with mental health difficulties. *The International Journal of Narrative Therapy and Community Work*, (4), 15–26.

Pluznick, R. & Kis-Sines, N. (2010, April). New narratives for parents with mental health difficulties. *Context Magazine*, 43–46.

Polanco, M., & Epston, D.(2009). Tales of travels across languages: Languages and their anti-languages. *The International Journal of Narrative Therapy and Community Work*, (4), 62–71.

Rose, N. (1993). *Governing the soul: The shaping of the private self.* London, England: Free Association Press.

Sax, P. (2008). *Re-authoring teaching: Creating a collaboratory.* Rotterdam/Taipei: Sense Publishers.

Sennett, R. (2000). *The corrosion of character: The personal consequences of work in the new capitalism.* New York, NY: W. W. Norton.

Simon, R. (Ed.) (1994). Psychotherapy's third wave? The promise of narrative [Special feature]. *The Family Therapy Networker, 18*(6), 18–49.

Sommer, D. (Ed.). (2003). *Bilingual games: Some literary investigations.* London, England: Palgrave Macmillan.

Sommer, D. (2004). *Bilingual aesthetics: A new sentimental education.* Durham, NC: Duke University Press.

Sudnow, D. (2001). *Ways of the hand: A rewritten account.* Boston, MA: The MIT Press.

Tamasese, K. & Waldegrave, C. (1993). Cultural and gender accountability in the "Just Therapy" approach. *Journal of Feminist Family Therapy, 5*(2), 29–45.

Tamasese, K., Waldegrave, C., Tuhaka, F., & Campbell, W. (1998). Furthering conversation about partnerships of accountability. *Dulwich Centre Journal,* (4), 50–62.

Taylor, C. (2007). *A secular age.* Cambridge, MA: Harvard University Press.

Vromans, L. P., & Schweitzer, R. D. (2010). Narrative therapy for adults with major depressive disorder: Improved symptom and interpersonal outcomes. *Psychotherapy Research,* 1–12. doi:10.1080 /10503301003591792

Vygotsky, L. (1986). *Thought and Language.* Cambridge, MA: MIT Press.

Waldegrave, C. (2005). "Just Therapy" with families on low incomes. *Child Welfare Journal, 84*(2), 265–276.

Waldegrave, C. (2009). Culture, gender and socio-economic contexts in therapeutic and social policy work. *Family Process, 48*(1), 85–101. doi:10.1111/j.1545–5300.2009.01269.x

Waldegrave, C., Tamasese, K., Tuhaka, F., & Campbell, W. (2003). *Just Therapy—a journey: A collection of papers from the Just Therapy Team, New Zealand.* Adelaide, Australia: Dulwich Centre Publications.

Welch, S. (1990). *A feminist ethic of risk.* Minneapolis, MN: Fortress Press.

Wever, C. (2009). Musical re-tellings: Songs, singing, and resonance in narrative practice. *The International Journal of Narrative Therapy and Community Work,* (3), 28–42.

White, M. (1984). Pseudo-encopresis: From avalanche to victory, from vicious to virtuous cycles. *Family Systems Medicine, 2*(2), 150–160. doi:10.1037/h0091651

White, M. (1988). Saying hullo again: The incorporation of the lost relationship in the resolution of grief. *Dulwich Centre Newsletter*, Spring, 7–11.

White, M. (1989a). Family therapy and schizophrenia: Addressing the "In-the-corner" lifestyle. In M. White, *Selected papers* (pp. 47–57). Adelaide, Australia: Dulwich Centre Publications.

White, M. (1989b). *Selected papers.* Adelaide, Australia: Dulwich Centre Publications.

White, M. (1989c). The process of questioning: A therapy of literary merit? In M. White, *Selected papers* (pp. 37–46). Adelaide, Australia: Dulwich Centre Publications. (Reprinted from *Dulwich Centre Newsletter*, 1988, Winter, 8–14).

White, M. (1992). Men's culture, the men's movement, and the constitution of men's lives. *Dulwich Centre Newsletter*, (3&4), 33–53.

White, M. (1993). Commentary: The histories of the present. In S. Gilligan & R. Price (Eds.), *Therapeutic conversations* (pp. 121–135). New York, NY: W. W. Norton.

White, M. (1994). A conversation about accountability (C. McLean, interviewer). *Dulwich Centre Newsletter*, (2&3), 68–79.

White, M. (1995a). *Re-authoring lives: Interviews and essays.* Adelaide, Australia: Dulwich Centre Publications.

White, M. (1995b). Reflecting teamwork as definitional ceremony. In M. White, *Re-authoring lives: Interviews and essays* (pp. 172–198). Adelaide, Australia: Dulwich Centre Publications.

White, M. (1997). *Narratives of therapists' lives.* Adelaide, Australia: Dulwich Centre Publications.

White, M. (2000a). Challenging the culture of consumption: Rites of passage and communities of acknowledgement. In M. White, *Reflections on narrative practice: Essays and interviews* (pp. 25–33). Adelaide, Australia: Dulwich Centre Publications. (Reprinted from *Dulwich Centre Newsletter*, 1997, [2&3], 38–42)

White, M. (2000b). *Reflections on narrative practice: Essays and interviews.* Adelaide, Australia: Dulwich Centre Publications.

White, M. (2001). Folk psychology and narrative practice [Special issue]. *Dulwich Centre Journal*, (2).

White, M. (2004). *Narrative practice and exotic lives: Resurrecting diversity in everyday life.* Adelaide, Australia: Dulwich Centre Publications.

White, M. (2007). *Maps of narrative practice.* New York, NY: W. W. Norton.

White, M., & Epston, D. (1990). *Narrative means to therapeutic ends.* New York, NY: W. W. Norton.

White, M., & Morgan, A. (2006). *Narrative therapy with children and their families.* Adelaide, Australia: Dulwich Centre Publications.

Wingard, B. (2010). A conversation with Lateral Violence. *The International Journal of Narrative Therapy and Community Work,* (1), 13–17.

Winslade, J. (2009). Tracing lines of flight: Implications in the work of Giles Deleuze for narrative practice. *Family Process, 48*(3), 332–346. doi:10.1111/j.1545–5300.2009.01286.x

Yuen, A., & White, C. (2007). *Conversations about gender, culture, violence & narrative practice: Stories of hope and complexity from women of many cultures.* Adelaide, Australia: Dulwich Centre Publications.

Index